Neural Networks

Step-by-Step

————— ❧❀❧ —————

Understand How Neural Networks Work,
Starting With Simple Ideas

Matthew Harper

Additionally, the information in the following pages is intended only for informational purposes and should thus be thought of as universal. As befitting its nature, it is presented without assurance regarding its prolonged validity or interim quality. Trademarks are mentioned without written consent and can in no way be considered an endorsement from the trademark holder.

Table of Contents

Introduction

Congratulations on downloading *Neural Networks Step-by-Step: Understand How Neural Networks work, Starting with Simple Ideas* and thank you for doing so.

The concept of artificial intelligence is definitely not a new one. The idea of a machine that can think for itself, make decisions, and plan its own course of actions have been burned into our consciousness from the time we were small children. No matter what your age or where you come from these thoughts inserted themselves into our minds decades ago.

It was first introduced to us through exciting TV shows as science fiction. The "What if" idea of a world where human beings are not the only ones with the capacity to observe their environment, analyze situations, make predictions, and decide on a course of action was initially a mere figment of someone's imagination. But isn't imagination the basis for every great idea that the world has ever embraced? Absolutely, and while it may have seemed unbelievable fifty or sixty years ago, the ability for a machine to do all of these things is not so far out of reach now. In fact, in many cases, the future is already here.

Throughout our history, mankind has created an array of amazing inventions that the world first witnessed through fearful eyes, which they later scrutinized with burning questions then caution, before finally embracing them.

Telephones were once thought of as conduits of evil spirits, yet today people can't leave home without them. Televisions were once thought to emit dangerous X-rays that could harm your health and make you go blind, yet nearly every household has at least one and most have several. When computers were first introduced, they were met with ridicule. Thomas Watson, the Chairman and CEO of IBM commented that "There is a world market for about five computers."

All of these inventions and countless more were not readily accepted by the masses. For many, it took decades for their true capabilities to be appreciated. Were people lacking in vision or did they not appreciate the potential that these wonderful devices had to offer? No. In time, they all came to realize the immense value these devices had. The problem was not lacking in vision nor was it their lack of understanding of what these things could do. Many who ridiculed these things saw first-hand how they worked.

The problem these new ideas faced was trying to get people to understand a device that was before its time. People could only see what was right in front of them and to promote a device, that's clearly meant for the future, in front of people who had never seen it before is rather difficult. No wonder the world ridiculed the idea of a machine thinking for itself because it seemed to be the stuff of fairy tales.

But a machine capable of learning is already here, it is real and it is exciting. Many may not be aware of it but it is already an important role in our lives in many ways. Ever wonder how all those lists of websites can come up so quickly when you do a Google search? What about how Amazon knows exactly what to recommend to you every time you visit their website? And what about how Netflix can choose a list of shows that suit your taste perfectly?

You didn't really think there were a bunch of people picking up your search request and creating these things on their own did you? The fact is that all of these things were done by artificial intelligence, machines programmed to do the grunt work for the masses. Basically, these are computers designed to perform certain functions that make our lives faster, efficient, and more convenient.

How these computers are capable of doing all of these things is the subject of this book. Using this book as a guide, we'll come to understand how the art of neural networks has made it possible for computer science to turn in a whole new direction, opening the doors to an amazing new era of technology. Even as a novice in this industry, you will understand the basics of what neural networks are, how they work, and the many tasks you can apply them to.

We live in exciting times, and the world as we know it is changing quickly. Machine learning is already a hot topic with amazing promises for everyone. It doesn't matter if you're planning to create your own neural network or if you're just attempting to get a better understanding of it. Our goal here is to give you all the information you need to understand how this technology is evolving and give you some guidelines to help you find your place in it. This way, you can decide for yourself whether you want to create your own neural network or if you just want to stand on the sidelines and reap the benefits of this amazing, ground-breaking technology.

There are plenty of books on this subject on the market, so thanks again for choosing this one! Every effort was made to ensure it is full of as much useful information as possible, please enjoy!

Chapter 1:
First, Machine Learning

D o you remember when you got your first computer? For most people, the device was so foreign to them they couldn't even understand what they were supposed to do with it. No doubt, for many people, they still wanted one even if they had no idea what its true purpose was. Even today, there are numerous people who have found computers nothing more than a great device for playing games, binge-watching their favorite TV shows, or streaming their favorite music.

But you can do so many amazing things if you know how to tap into the true potential of these wonderful devices. Once a person knows what to do with modern day machines, things begin to change in very big ways. We can easily take a task and go beyond the basics. When that happens, computers become far more than a glorified calculator that can decipher calculations and numbers in a fraction of a second. To get to that point there are a few things that you must understand.

Machines now do not have to have every detail of their functions automatically programmed. They can be programmed to learn a number of tasks and make the necessary adjustments to perform the functions that will allow them to work more efficiently.

Frankly, there are certain computer functions that many assume to be advanced technology but are merely things that can be done very quickly. For example, at the heart of every computer is a very complex calculator. When the computer performs an action we think is fascinating, it is merely the machine performing a number of mathematical equations to produce the results we desire.

You might want to stream your favorite movie to your computer. You click a few buttons and in a matter of seconds, scenes begin to play out in front of your eyes. Really, this function is nothing more than the computer running a bunch of basic math problems in the background, taking the sums and reconstructing them into a video on your screen.

The formulas used are pretty basic, most of them are not different from what you learned in high school. The difference is that computers can do them much faster than we can with our human minds. Even if we are the best at figuring out these types of math problems, humans can never calculate them as quickly as a computer can. Our minds aren't built that way. While it may take us a minute or so to calculate a few numbers in our head, computers have the capability of figuring out millions of equations in a fraction of the time.

But that does not mean that computers are an improved version of the human mind. There are things that the human mind can do equally fast that computers have yet to figure out. Actions like pattern recognition, unstructured problem solving and functioning in 3-dimensional space. Yes, more advanced computers can perform these types of tasks and solve problems, but they have to be given structure and parameters in areas where rules must be followed. Human minds are flexible enough to adapt their thinking to varying circumstances in a vast array of areas. Yes, computers can operate cars and come to quick conclusions, but they have difficulty multitasking and maneuvering in areas without bumping into things or encountering an error.

However, with each passing year, the latest computers are capable of doing more and more things that they could never do in the past. It seems to be just a matter of time before they will one day be capable of doing everything that humans can do but much faster and far more efficiently.

This may seem like science fiction but the possibility is all too real, thanks to the creation of neural networks. In its simplest of terms, neural networks are a series of mathematical formulas called algorithms that identify relationships in a group of data. The network can accomplish this by mimicking the human brain and how it works.

These are complicated networks that are capable of adapting to constantly changing data so that it can achieve the best results possible without having to redesign the criteria needed to get the optimum output.

To put it more simply, neural networks are the means of injecting flexibility into a computer system so that it processes data in a way that is similar to how the human brain works. Of course, computers are still going to be made in the same way as other machines but with each improvement, they are getting closer and closer to thinking machines rather than devices that are strictly following a static set of instructions.

Before we can fully understand neural networks, we have to get a firm grasp on what we mean when we talk about a machine that can learn. We are not talking about giving machines textbooks, homework, and exams so they can learn in the same way a student does. That would be ridiculous, but it helps to see just how a computer can mimic the human brain. So, let's look at how the human brain works first and make a comparison.

When a human being absorbs new information, they usually gain the information from something they're not familiar with. It could come in the form of a question or a statement of something new, or it could come as an experience with no verbal connection whatsoever. The information is picked up through the body's five senses and transmitted directly to the brain. The brain then reshuffles a number of its neural pathways (we call this thinking) so it can process the information and then when all the details related to the information is compared and analyzed in the brain, an answer or a conclusion is drawn and instructions are sent out to the rest of the body.

Since computers don't really think, they have to accomplish the same goal but in a different way. Information is inputted into the computer's programming, it is then processed, calculated, and analyzed based on a number of preset algorithms, and then a conclusion, prediction, or answer is drawn and it comes out as output.

Let's look at an example. Let's say you want to figure out the answer to the problem 7 - 6. This is a basic math question that will require you to 'think' in order to get the right answer. While we will do this very quickly, we need to understand what is happening in our brain so we can see the similarity with computers.

When we receive information, our senses automatically send all the data relating to it to the brain. The brain is made up of billions of neurons that are all interconnected, creating miles upon miles of pathways where information can travel. What's really neat about our brain is that these pathways are constantly shifting based on the data that is being transmitted. When new information is received, they will shift to create new pathways to transmit it to where it needs to go in the brain. Throughout this process, this shifting will continue until a solution is decided upon. Then instructions are sent throughout the body's central nervous system to different parts of the body instructing them on the proper way to respond to the information received. The brain accomplishes all of this in fractions of a second.

In a neural network, the same thing happens. While these networks cannot perfectly mimic the inner workings of the brain, the process is very similar. The information is taken in and the neural network does all the work of consuming data, processing it, and coming up with a workable solution. These networks allow the computer to 'learn' by using algorithms.

What are algorithms?

No doubt, you've heard the term before. It is often associated with all sorts of technical mechanics but in recent years algorithms are being used in the development of automatic learning, the field that is leading us to advancements in artificial and computational intelligence. This is a method of analyzing data in a way that makes it possible for machines to analyze and process data. With this type of data, computers can work out and perform a number of tasks it could not originally do. They can understand different concepts, make choices, and predict possibilities for the future.

To do this, the algorithms have to be flexible enough to adapt and make adjustments when new data is presented. They are therefore able to give the needed solution without having to create a specific code to solve a problem. Instead of programming a rigid code into the system, the relevant data becomes part of the algorithm which in turn, allows the machine to create its own reasoning based on the data provided.

How does this work?

This might sound a little confusing but we'll try to break this down into certain examples you can relate to. One of the 'learning' functions of machines is the ability to classify information. To do this, the input data can be a mix of all types of information. The algorithm needs to identify the different elements of the data and then group them into several different categories based on characteristics of similarities, differences, and other factors.

These characteristics can be any number of things ranging from identifying handwriting samples to the types of documents received. If this were code, the machine could only do one single function but because it is an algorithm which can be altered to fit a wide variety of things, the computer can receive this data and classify all sorts of groups that fit within the specific parameters of the circumstances.

This is how machines can change their functions to adapt to the situation at hand. Your email account can analyze all the emails you received, based on a pattern that you have followed, and it divides them into different groups. It can identify which emails are important and you should see right away, those that are spam and junk mail, and even sort out those that may pose a risk to your computer because it carries a virus or malware.

With these types of algorithms, machines can now learn by observing your habits and patterns and adjust their behavior accordingly. So, the very secret to a successful and effective neural pathway depends a great deal on the algorithms your system uses.

Types of algorithms

Without algorithms, machines cannot learn. So, over the years many different ones have been developed. Depending on what you want your machine to do, they can be grouped into two different categories: supervised and unsupervised.

Supervised

A supervised algorithm requires a detailed input of related data over a period of time. Once all the information is available to the computer, it is used to classify any new data relating to it. The computer then does a series of calculations, comparisons, and analysis before it makes a decision.

This type of algorithm requires an extensive amount of information to be programmed into the system so that the computer can make the right decision. That way, when it needs to solve a problem, it will attempt to determine which mathematical function it needs to use in order to find the correct solution. With the right series of algorithms already programmed into the system, the machine can sift through all types of data in order to find the solution to a wide variety of problems in the related category.

Supervised algorithms are referred that way because they require human input to ensure that the computer has the right data to process the information it receives.

Unsupervised

An unsupervised algorithm implies that the computer does not have all the information to make a decision. Maybe it has some of the data needed but one or two factors may be missing. This is kind of like the algebra problems you encountered in school. You may have two factors in the problem but you must solve the third on your own. $A + b = c$. If you know A but you have no idea what b is then you need to plug the information into an equation to solve the problem.

With unsupervised learning, this can be an extremely complex type of problem to solve. For this type of problem, you'll need an algorithm that recognizes various elements of a problem and can incorporate that into the equation. Another type of algorithm will look for any inconsistencies in the data and try to solve the problem by analyzing those.

Unsupervised algorithms clearly are much more complex than the supervised algorithms. While they may start with some data to solve a problem, they do not have all the information so they must be equipped with the tools to find those missing elements without having a human to provide all the pieces of the puzzle for them.

Aside from the two major types of algorithms, there are a number of other types that might be used to teach a machine to learn.

Reinforcement learning

This type of algorithm allows the system to interact with the environment in an effort to attain a certain goal. Reinforcement learning is commonly used in video games where the computer must navigate and adjust its movements in order to win the game. A reward system is used so the computer knows and understands when it should make the right move, but there are also negative consequences whenever they make errors. This type of algorithm works best in situations where the computer has an obstacle that it must overcome like a rival in a game, or it could also be a self-driving car that needs to reach its destination. The entire focus of the computer is to accomplish certain tasks while navigating the unpredictable environment around it. With each mistake, the computer will readjust its moves in order to reduce the number of errors so it can achieve the desired result.

Semi-supervised learning

Semi-supervised learning is a blend of both supervised and reinforcement learning. The computer is given an incomplete set of data from which to work. Some of the data include specific examples of previous decisions made with the available data while other data is missing completely. These algorithms work on solving a specific problem or performing very specific functions that will help them achieve their goals.

Of course, these are not the only algorithms that can be used in a computer program to help the machine learning. But, the general idea is the same. The algorithm must fit with the problem the computer needs to solve.

With artificial neural networks applying these different 'secret formulas' many computers can perform functions, solve problems, and carry on a vast variety of learning processes they could not be capable of doing. This field of computer programming is termed 'deep learning,' a subset of machine learning that makes up the foundation of the material contained in this book.

Chapter 2:
What Is a Neural Network?

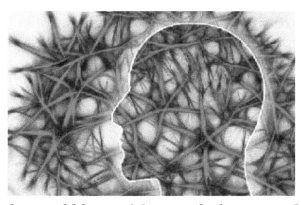

We have already pointed out that these algorithms are an integral part of machine learning. They are used to sift through all sorts of data, pull out any information that could be useful to reach the targeted goal and bring you to the closest possible solution to a problem. All of this is done without having to write a specific code for the computer to actually solve the problem because of something called a 'neural network.'

But what exactly is a neural network? Let's go back and take another look at the human brain so we can get a better understanding of this new technology.

The brain holds billions of tiny little neurons that are poised to receive data and process it. These neurons are all interconnected through a complex web with each neuron holding a certain amount of information. These neurons send signals to each other as they process the data they receive.

In a computer, a neural network is created artificially. The architecture has been around for decades but the technology has advanced enough just recently for it to be implemented into any usable and functional form.

In an artificial neural network (ANN) these neurons are mimicked by thousands (sometimes millions) of tiny little processing units, all linked together. Each one of these artificial neurons has a purpose, which is determined by the configuration or the topology of the network.

There are several layers of these neurons and each layer has its own specific purpose. There is the input layer, where all the data flows into the network, the output layer where the solution is produced, and there could be numerous hidden layers where much of the processing work is done.

The concepts behind neural networks

Back when these networks were originally created, the structures were much simpler than they are today. They consisted of only a few internal units while in today's technological age, each network could literally have millions of tiny little units each perfectly capable of understanding and mastering extremely complex patterns to function properly. The combined efforts of all of these nodes make it possible for the computer to analyze the data it receives, process it, find any type of inconsistencies, and produce a satisfactory result.

We already understand that computers use processors and memory to perform complex computations very quickly. The problem with this system is that they are not capable of adapting to varying forms of input. By utilizing neural networks, computers now have an alternative means of addressing problems.

Their underlying concept can be easily understood when it is compared to the way the physical brain works. In a physical human brain, there is an internal computer that holds approximately 10^{11} tiny little transistors. These are small little switches that can turn on or off on command. They respond very quickly to input data with a switching time of around 10^3 seconds, which is incredibly fast.

Our brains receive and process information in three stages. The senses are feeding the brain with information on a continuous basis. It never stops as shown in the diagram below.

Sense organs receive information through taste, sight, touch, smell, and sound Information is then sent to the central nervous system, which consists of the brain and/or the spinal cord Information is processed and instructions are sent to other parts of the body to produce an appropriate response

As you can see, information is continually flowing in one direction. But the function of a physical neural network is much more complicated. A neural network is an attempt to recreate this process in computers. The diagram above, of course, is a highly simplified view of how the brain works. In reality, it is highly complex in how it operates and consists of many parts that all work in harmony in order to accurately simulate thought and learning.

A neural network does not even come close to duplicating the learning process of the brain but its function is based on the basic fundamentals of how the brain operates.

In a typical biological neural network, the key components are the neurons. In a computer system, these are referred to as units (or nodes). Each of these nodes can:

- Receive input from other neurons within its network

- Adapt its internal state to the data received

- Duplicate or create a response signal to send to other neurons within the network

When a neuron receives data, it is transmitted through a series of electrical impulses. The data is encoded based on the period and the recurrence of each of these impulses. In a biological neural network, one neuron can be directly connected to as many as 10,000 other neurons, with each neuron establishing its own pathways and the flow of information based on the impulses received. An artificial neural network attempts to achieve the same results by making the same type of adaptive changes through simulation. To help understand this process, let's have a look at the different components of a neural network in action:

- **Input**

  Input is data received from the external environment. This could be a pattern, a word, or an image. This data is entered into the system and is mathematically designated by the notation X_i *for* I in *{1, n}* where n equals the number of inputs.

- **Weights**

  Weights show the strength of the connections between the neurons within the neural network. Every piece of data input must be multiplied by the weights, designated by the symbol w_i. After the inputs are all weighed, they are then summed up within the artificial neuron.

- **Sum**

  The sum is given a numerical value, which can range anywhere from zero to infinity. However, the computer will have to limit the response to a set of parameters in order to arrive at a workable value. To accomplish this, a threshold value is established and the sum must be put through an activation function, which is responsible for adjustments based on the data, allowing it to be transformed into the desired output.

Activation functions

The final stage of processing in an artificial neural network is the activation function where it will take the weighted sum of the input data, add bias, then determine whether or not the data is applicable to the problem and should be used or not.

Basically, the **weighted Sum + Bias** determines the importance of the data to the problem the machine is trying to solve. So, how does the machine determine this? By analyzing the value produced by a neuron to decide if any outside connections should view the neuron as 'fired' or not. Let's try to see this in action:

$$Y = \sum (weight * input) + bias$$

Here, the value of Y can be any value from *-infinity to +infinity*. At this point, the neuron does not know the limits of the value which means it won't be able to decide if the neuron should be fired or not. In the biological brain, electronic impulses will fire when a neuron should be stimulated because of the data it receives. In other words, it activates.

In a computer, this same process is done through several steps:

- A threshold is established. If the value of Y is above this threshold, it is declared activated. If it falls below this threshold, it will not.

If Y > threshold = A (activated)

This type of formula is referred to as a 'step function.' If the output is 1, the neuron is activated when the value is > o (threshold) and if the output is o it is not activated.

This works well in many cases but not always. This function works best when dealing with strictly 'yes or no' questions. However, in more advanced machines, there may be a need to introduce multiple neurons to connect in order to bring in more classifications of data. In that case, this system would be too basic. It may activate too many neurons, making it very difficult to come up with the best solution to the task.

Ideally, the computer should only activate one neuron to properly solve the problem. In this case, you would need a function that works at activating several different neurons and then choosing those neurons that showed the highest activation rate in comparison to the others.

In a case such as this, a linear function is better suited.

$A = cx$

This type of activation function is based on a straight line where activation is measured in proportion to the input. With this formula, if several neurons activate, the computer can get a range where they can connect them together and then choose the one that has the maximum activation.

But even this formula won't work in every case. There will be situations where there are connected layers and if each layer is activated using this formula, the activation will be passed on to the next level using the result of this formula as an input. That means that no matter how many layers there are they could be replaced by a single layer. In essence, the benefit of the layers and their computations will be invalid. The result will always be the same as with a single layer.

To avoid this problem, there is the sigmoid activation function.

$A - 1/1 + e^{-x}$

This type of activation function is nonlinear in nature. The combinations it uses are also nonlinear. It works better when stacking layers. It is also non-binary, so it will provide an analog activation that is different from a step function.

When X values range from -2 *to* 2, the Y values can be very steep. This means that any small changes in the value of X in that region of the network will automatically cause the values of Y to change as well. This means that the function is very likely to bring the Y values to either edge of the curve, making it a good classifier. This formula is great for creating clear distinctions on predictions.

This is probably why the sigmoid function is one of the most widely accepted functions in use today. But even it has problems.

As you can see, there have to be quite a few different activation functions used in order to ensure that the output of a neural network yields the results needed. Because of the constant variation of data received, there are many different formulas that will allow the computer to learn from its environment.

Since all these activation functions work with different types of data, it can be difficult to know which formula to use. If the system knows the characteristics of the data, it can easily choose the activation function that will yield the results faster. But as the data makes its way through the network, several functions have to be applied until the computer gives the most accurate result.

Architectures

As we begin to understand neural networks better, we begin to formulate an image of a very distinct architecture. Each network has very specific components that are arranged in layers. Most of them have a three-layered architecture but some can have even more.

Layers

A neural network is divided up into three or more layers, each having a completely different function. These layers are stacked up on top of each other and join up with each other during the artificial learning process.

Input layers

This is where the data is received. The nodes on the input are passive in the sense that they do not have a function that will allow them to modify data. Their sole purpose is to receive the data from their external environment.

Output layers

These are responsible for making computations and communicating instructions to the outside environment.

Hidden layers

A neural network could have one hidden layer or it could have hundreds. Their role is to copy the information the input layer receives and disseminate it to other layers in the network. They also perform calculations and exchange data taken from the input hubs and deliver it to the yield hubs.

Most neural networks are completely interconnected so that every neuron is connected to every other neuron on the previous layer before it and to the layer above it. This way, the input layer is always connected to the hidden layer, and the hidden layer is always connected to the output layer.

This layering is also found in the human brain. However, the human brain literally contains billions of neurons fully interconnected whereas a computer system may only have thousands or millions at the most. It is this unique architecture that makes it possible for computers to mimic the thinking process and actually learn new information without having to have all the data entered into their programs.

Chapter 3:
Technical Fields and How They Operate

Even the most advanced neural networks are pretty primitive when compared to the human brain. They tend to process information one at a time whereas the biological brain can easily multitask, capable of doing several things at once and that's all without having to burn extra energy to get it done.

Think of what you do every day. You can prepare a meal, have a conversation, and fill out your shopping list all at the same time. If you work in an office, you may be typing a letter, taking phone calls, and doing research altogether. In comparison, the artificial neural networks generally 'learn' by comparing one classification of a record with another classification. When there are errors that result from this process, they will readjust their formula and modify the algorithm and repeat the process, each time reducing the rate of error until they find a solution that best matches the task at hand.

Training the neural network

Let's look at this process in a bit more detail. First by looking at what a neural network is really comprised of.

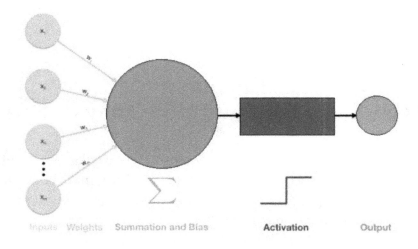

1. A set of input values and their weights.

2. A function that calculates the sum of the weights and then maps the results to an output

These two elements and how they work together can be seen clearly in the diagram below.

As you can see, the neurons on the input level receive the data input. The hidden layer directly above the input layer copies the data and any weights associated with it. Then these sums are totaled up and measured against known biases before the data is passed on to an activation layer where the decision will be made to fire the neuron or not. If the neuron is fired, then an appropriate output is determined, which will send a signal to the external environment dictating what action, if any, should be taken.

To visualize this better, it helps to know that there are no physical neurons on the different layers but rather a compilation of coded values contained in a data record. The next layer or series of layers are the hidden layers, where most of the computations will be performed, and the final layer or the output layer contains a single node for each class. As the data passes through the network, every node in the output layer is assigned a specific value, and the record is awarded to the node that contains the highest value.

In supervised training, during the training phase, each record has a known value so the output nodes can be assigned the correct values. A "1" is assigned to the node with the correct class and a "0" for all the others. This way, the computer can compare the calculated values with the correct values and determine the percentage of error for each node. This is called the Delta Rule.

The delta rule

Sometimes referred to as the 'least mean square method,' the delta rule is probably the most commonly used rule in training a neural network. With every input vector, the system compares the output vector to the correct solution. If the difference is 0, it means that the system learned nothing in the process. If the value is anything other than zero, the system automatically goes back to the weights associated with the input data and makes adjustments to bring the difference closer to zero.

For example, if you wanted to calculate the answer for 3 x 4, the computer will likely process the information as 4 + 4 + 4 and give you an output of 12. This is pretty basic thinking and both human brains and neural networks can get the result in a matter of seconds. However, let's suppose the problem is a bit more complex.

Perhaps we don't know the right formula to calculate the right answer. All we know is that the information is linear, which means that if one number in the equation is doubled, the other number must also be doubled. In a biological brain, this type of linear thinking is called 'intuition.'

The relationship between the different factors gives an indication of what needs to be done. The computer will apply an equation which reflects that relationship to solve the problem.

The only other data the system will have could be some examples that multiply numbers together to get the correct value. This data stored in the memory banks give real evidence that shows exactly how to arrive at the correct answer. The program will then process that calculation and compare it to the data it already has. If the difference is off, it will go back and make adjustments and then recalculate to solve for a better answer. It will continue to do this until it gets an answer that is either exact or close enough that it cannot reduce the error rate any longer.

The network 'learns' by checking the error rate and continuously readjusting until it gets to the right solution. This continuous refinement of the answer as a means to get to the nearest point of the correct answer is the simplest form of training the neural network.

There are many algorithms that are already programmed into the system that can be called upon to find the right solution to a given problem. These algorithms are chosen based on the type of problem the computer needs to solve.

Clustering

But how can we get a network to classify data rather than calculate it? This simply requires using a different type of algorithm. Let's say you have images of dogs and birds all mixed together and you want the computer to separate those images. In a biological brain, you can tell in a fraction of a second which ones are cats and which ones are dogs, but this is something a computer can't do.

This almost the same general process of repeating the algorithm and constantly refining the answer until you have successfully completed the task. However, in the case of classification, the network doesn't need to come up with some type of mathematical theory to solve the problem. Instead, it relies on some examples to guide its choices.

The data received may detail specific characteristics of dogs and birds. These are characteristics that are common knowledge and everyone knows to be true. These details are referred to as the 'training data.' Of course, the data needs to be in a language that the computer can understand. Descriptions such as "A dog has four legs, a tail, and pointed ears" will not do. Instead, the input data will be in the form of a table or a graph.

Example	Width	Length	Features	Classification
1	6" - 24'	1' - 5'	Hair	Dog
2	2" - 2'	5" - 3'	Feathers	Bird

The network will use this set of examples to plot a slope separating any data that matches the criteria. It will begin with a random division so that it has a baseline to work with. It will then check its answers against the known truths it already has to see how close it is to the correct division. Then it will repeat the process over and over again until it reaches the right solution. This process is called 'clustering' and is used for classifying different things, and for making predictions based on data received.

Once the correct result is attained, the data is stored in the memory banks and is used as an example the next time another problem like this comes up. In this way, the computer actually 'learns.'

These are not the only ways a neural network can learn but as you can see from the examples, the process is very basic. It is important, however, to understand that when the system has to figure out a problem with multiple elements in it, each hidden layer in the network can only perform one function. So, an extremely complex problem may require many hidden layers in order to come up with the right solution.

To put it simply, these programs cannot read words so basic mathematical algorithms are used to determine the relationship between the output error of a problem and the correct answer (or a solution that will solve the problem). This process is repeated over and over again, refining the answer until it reaches a point where it cannot be improved any further. In order for this to be accomplished, the neural network must be set up with real-world examples of data that is known to be true and accurate. If the data the system relies on is not accurate it is not possible for the computer to learn and expand that knowledge.

Chapter 4:
What Is It Used for and How?

There is a great deal of excitement surrounding this new technology. With each new advancement, machine learning is gradually moving closer towards handling the more abstract tasks that up until now, have only been successfully done by humans. It is difficult to convince those who are not familiar with the science of the many tasks that machine learning can accomplish.

The different ways this can be used are endless. In fact, there are probably quite a few applications that are affecting your life right now that you didn't realize were being implemented.

Deep learning

Even without a background in computer science, one can understand what the term 'machine learning is.' Basically, it is a machine that learns from data. As long as the machine has the right data input there is a huge number of problems that it can solve without any human interference. As long as the machine is given the correct training data and the right algorithms, it can perform the necessary functions and continue to learn from them for an indefinite period of time.

The primary tools at the heart of deep learning are the input data and algorithms. Without the correct data, it is not possible for deep learning to take place. For years, machines have functioned without algorithms but these machines are programmed to perform certain functions without change (think vending machines) which means the program it started out with will not adapt over time. It will still perform the same actions over and over again regardless of the environment that surrounds it.

However, with deep learning, the computer is capable of making continuous adjustments in order to improve its performance every time it is used. But to really grasp the concept of deep learning, we need to take some time and look closely under the hood. Its use today can help us to see how deep learning is already changing our lives for the better.

When we turn on our home PCs we automatically expect things to happen, and we expect them to happen at record speeds without even thinking about what goes into getting the results we want.

When you turn on Netflix, you will quickly see a list of movies, documentaries, and TV shows that you like. You make your choice without thinking about how deep learning machines have studied your choices over the years and came up with options that are more appealing to you. If you like science fiction, miraculously, you will have a host of science fiction options laid out before you. Because the machine has analyzed your entertainment choices you have the best options in front of you to choose from.

Deep learning is also used by Google, to predict what websites you will most likely want to visit. Google's voice and image recognition algorithms are being used in a host of new industries. MIT is now using deep learning to predict events that are most likely to happen in the future. Everywhere you look, deep learning is beginning to permeate all types of industries and expectations are that it will continue to grow in the future.

But for those who don't fully grasp computer science concepts, the thought of deep learning might instill fear instead of excitement. After all, in the past few decades, the subject has been approached with a lot of skepticism and doubt. Movies have portrayed power hungry machines bent on taking over the world, and news reports about every self-functioning machine failure have been exploited to the highest level. It leads some people to believe that machines capable of learning are more of a threat to humanity than a help. So, what exactly is this kind of technology used for and do we really have anything to worry about?

Classification

Deep learning machines have extremely comprehensive databases and sophisticated networks that allow for easy classification of many different forms of data. We might assume that looking at a picture and identifying its contents is pretty basic stuff. To the human eye, images can be classified in a fraction of a second but to a machine, which only sees things in terms of math, they contain many different elements that must first be sorted out.

Deep learning, however, makes it possible for machines to classify any type of data including video, speech, audio, or handwriting and analyze it to come up with a conclusion that would be similar to that of most humans.

Imagine a computer system that can automatically create a record of the number of vehicles that pass through a certain point on a public road during a set time frame. The steps needed for this to happen are immense. Not only would it have to hold a huge database of different types of cars, their shapes, and sizes but it must also capable of processing the data and analyzing it to come up with an acceptable answer.

Comparing the data it receives through its sensors to the data it has stored in the database, it can classify the answer with a pretty high level of accuracy. While humans could easily identify cars by make and model, the idea of having a human standing on a street corner counting and labeling cars would virtually be impossible to achieve. Even if someone could position themselves to count, humans get tired and need to have frequent breaks. They cannot function continuously without stopping. The level of accuracy would be much lower. Yet, automobile manufacturers, government agencies, and other industries could find the information extremely valuable in making decisions for their business.

But deep learning goes even further than this. While the system may already be programmed with a massive database, as the machine operates it will learn even more and increase its knowledge from its experiences. By being programmed to train itself, continuous human interaction is not necessary. The machine will learn from its mistakes in much the same way as humans do.

Pattern recognition

Pattern recognition is probably the oldest form of machine learning but is also the most fundamental. As of 2015, pattern recognition was one of the most popular areas of interest in research labs around the globe. By giving a machine the ability to recognize a character or some other object, the potential for machine learning increased exponentially.

The ability of a machine to recognize handwritten numbers and letters opens the door to a myriad of uses. This ability has been successful in providing insights into the complex movements of the environment, weather changes, and even in the world of finance. But deep learning involves more than just identifying similar characteristics and differences in images. Pattern recognition allows them to draw their own conclusions in regards to the images or videos they are analyzing and tagging them appropriately. Every time they perform this type of analysis, the better it will become at identifying similar situations and unusual anomalies that could affect the outcome.

Right now, the New York City Department of Transportation has joined up with IntelliScape.io to use this technology and get a better understanding of traffic in their area. They can now see patterns in the weather, identify areas where parking violations are more likely to occur, and as a result, inform local officials of these patterns so they can be prepared to respond accordingly.

There are many uses for pattern recognition in many areas. It can be used to expand the 'Internet of Things' by collecting data from any device that is connected to the internet. Cities will use it to understand how people navigate through their streets, urban planners can make better decisions about the location of physical infrastructures and even in the area of conservation, it can be helpful. Instead of using manpower to go out and count trees, drones can be deployed to analyze the number of trees and their health in any given area.

Prediction

The use of predictions can also be used by many industries. Whether it is in the field of medicine to detect abnormal genes in an unborn child or predicting the change in weather, because of the ability of these machines to paint a realistic picture of future possibilities their potential is huge.

Industries are already using this prediction technology in a vast number of fields.

The pharmaceutical industry uses it to determine the exact set of compounds needed to treat a specific disease. They can now predict which medicines will be more effective and use that data to develop new drugs to fight disease. They can also use it to identify alternative treatments that may also be effective.

In the area of cybersecurity, programs like Deep Instinct focuses on predicting where cyber hackers and other online threats may occur so they can develop ways of protecting the end user before an attack actually happens.

In agriculture, crop outputs can be determined even before planting begins. The computer will analyze weather predictions, soil conditions, and quality of seeds to determine how successful a crop will be and how much profit can be gained.

The same can be said in areas of retail, insurance, finance, and even in aerospace. The potential for this type of technology is vast and positive. As more and more industries begin to adopt deep learning and incorporate it into their business strategies, all sorts of events will become much more efficient and accurate.

Years ago, this type of technology was thought to be in the realm of science fiction and fantasy, but today it is a reality. While computers are a long way from the kind of independent thinking and autonomy that could rule the world, they definitely have come a long way from the vending machine era. The future of neural networks and deep learning are extremely progressive and definitely something we can all look forward to with high anticipation.

Chapter 5:
Types of Neural Networks

U p until now, we've discussed the basic principles that support neural networks but you've probably gathered that there is a lot more to it than the basics. There are, in fact, many different types of neural networks, each designed to address a specific type of problem. In this chapter, we'll look at some of these neural networks in order to get a better understanding of their purpose and how they are used.

Convolutional neural networks

For humans, image recognition is done without thought. It happens almost instantly. We see a photo of our grandmother and we don't have to analyze it to determine who it is, we just know. Every person can identify a bird when they see one. In our brains, this process is second nature but teaching a computer to do it is no easy task.

Computers can do this now with the use of a convolutional neural network. This is a neural network that uses identical replicas of the same neuron. This makes it possible for the network to learn the characteristics of a single neuron and then use it in a variety of different places.

The architecture of a convolutional neural network is based on the biological process that happens when a person identifies something with their sight. In the human eye, individual cortical neurons respond to stimulation from light as it enters the person's field of vision. This is known as the 'receptive field,' which is almost entirely covered by neurons. In a computer, this process is accomplished with convolutional neural networks (CNN).

These are a special class of networks that are enhanced to be extremely powerful in selected fields like image recognition and classification. They can identify objects, signs, and are the primary tool used in modern inventions like self-driving automobiles.

Each CNN has several sub-sampling layers as well as a number of additional layers that are all interconnected. When data input is gathered it is based on a very specific formula that tells the computer the height and the width of the image as well as the number of colors and any other characteristics that will allow the computer to make an identification.

To create a CNN, the computer must be programmed to recognize an object. Any object. Just like with other types of neural networks, computers can solve a number of different problems by linking a series of neurons together. This way, all the neurons work together to calculate the relevant features of the problem. With a CNN, you can use the same algorithms but adapt them to different types of problems. By adapting the algorithm to recognize an object rather than coming up with a numerical calculation you can simplify the task.

CNN's can only work with data, the more data it receives the easier it will accomplish the task. If you want the computer to identify a handwriting sample, it is important to provide it with a large number of handwriting samples to use as a basis for its assumption.

To that end, researchers have already created a dataset of handwritten numbers called the MNIST, which contains more than 60,000 images of handwritten figures. However, computers only recognize numerical values not images, so you will have to transform those images into a matrix of numbers, which symbolizes its different characteristics.

To input this image into a neural network it needs to be transformed from a visual image to a matrix that consists of more than 300 numbers, which should look something like this:

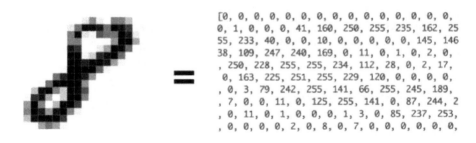

In order to manage all of these inputs, the neural network must be expanded so that it has at least 2 outputs instead of 1. The first output will calculate the probability rate that the picture is a 'number 8' while the other output will do the opposite and calculate the probability that the image is not. The system will then categorize all the images in the database with a separate output for each group of items it will have to identify.

While the neural network is not capable of matching the recognition skills of the human eye, it can recognize objects when properly programmed to do so. This type of function can be very useful in a wide range of industries that need recognition skills in areas where humans cannot function at an extremely rapid pace.

Perceptron and backpropagation

The most basic and simplest form of a neural network is the perceptron. It has a simple binary function that can produce only two possible results. If the solution it produces is positive the function will produce a 1 but if it is negative the result will be a 0.

This type of network is designed for a very specific class of problems, such as the identification of objects. A single perceptron can identify a dividing line and can tell whether any given point is located above or below that line.

Multilayer perceptron

Multilayer perceptrons are often used to analyze a large amount of data that exists in table format. They can decipher rows and columns and use them as variables. This system works best when the rows and columns are interchangeable. They can switch them around without risk of changing the meaning or the value of the data.

In an MLP, the input for the classifier is first changed by using a non-linear transformation formula. This places the input data into an area where it can then be separated linearly. This is usually done in one of the hidden layers of the network.

To train an MLP, parameters must be set. These parameters must represent the qualities of the classifications that need to be made. The good news is that in the last few decades, guidelines have been created that make selecting these parameters much simpler. Several of these guidelines already exist and can be found in programs like the Efficient BackProp.

Backpropagation

Backpropagation was originally introduced back in the 70s but was not fully put to use until later in the 80s. It is a faster method than many other neural networks of its time. It is an algorithm that can be used in supervised learning in many artificial neural networks and can be used to create a gradient descent and as a means of training neural networks.

The method does a calculation to determine the gradient of the error function in relation to the weights. Basically, the concept is that the gradient will move backward through the network so that the last layer of weights is calculated first and those of the first layer are calculated last.

Training with backpropagation uses the gradient descent technique in order to find the updates of the weights. Gradient descent is basically the trial and error method where the rate of error is minimized with each successive iteration (or attempt) in order to lower the percentage of error.

Backpropagation calculates the delta rule when using a multilayer feed-forward network and requires three components:

- A dataset, which comprises input/output pairs

- Feedforward neural networks

- And an error function

The network is trained to give an estimation of the value of a specific function. The system is trained using the dataset to identify a pattern. Afterward, the network will need to give an estimate of the value using the Gaussian function to make an approximation.

To make a time series prediction, the goal is to develop a network that can predict a value on a given time series. This type of network is often used in making stock market predictions or to analyze market trends. In such cases, the input data is given in chunks and the output it yields will become the next piece of data that follows that chunk.

There are, of course, several other types of neural networks that can be applied to a wide number of problem-solving issues. Based on the network's given architecture, the algorithms used, and the quality of the data input, these networks can be applied to a vast number of conditions.

Whether the goal is to identify certain images or to calculate large numbers to come up with a prediction, there is a good chance that the type of neural network needed is already in existence.

Chapter 6:
Neural Networks and Artificial Intelligence

Probably the most exciting application of neural networks is its use in artificial intelligence. This sub-niche is the reason why many are waiting in anticipation for the future. While there is no specific definition of this type of technology, almost everyone you meet will have an opinion of what artificial intelligence really means.

Actually, artificial intelligence is a form of science with the primary goal of developing machines that have the ability to continuously increase their intelligence. It is a progressive science that is only made possible because of the creation of neural networks. To do this, scientists must constantly improve on the networks with each new creation. They hope that the machines will get closer and closer to a level of intelligence comparable to humans.

Only humans have the ability to think, analyze, and understand their environment, its actions, and the realities that exist. Only humans can explain their world and think in the abstract. Our brains can take in a wealth of information and draw conclusions in the fraction of a second.

Machines, on the other hand, using the same set of data, will face numerous challenges. For example, today, computers can hold a database of thousands of similar images, assess them and draw a conclusion with 95% efficiency. This is quite impressive by any stretch but still, it cannot explain why it chose the images, ascertain their meaning, or distinguish why one image is different from another. In other words, computers can compute but they can't reason. So, even though they are capable of producing amazing results with the tasks they are given, they still are far behind the ability of the human brain in many ways.

To overcome these obstacles, a unique form of machine learning has been developed. Most of us know it as Artificial Intelligence or AI. The term refers to the simulation of intelligence in machines. Today's machines are programmed to 'think' and mimic the way the human brain operates. These machines are slowly taught to rationalize in given situations, analyze, and choose a course of action that would have the best chance of achieving the optimum goal.

As technology continues to advance, it is only natural that older machines will become outdated. For example, machines that perform basic functions or can recognize and identify text used to be cutting edge but today, they are so obsolete that they are no longer considered to be an artificial intelligence. This is because the function now is taken for granted. This ability has become so commonplace that it is often viewed as a normal computer function.

Computers said to have artificial intelligence today are those that show more impressive abilities like being able to play chess, self-driving cars, and smart homes. Why are these functions given the label of artificial intelligence? For those that can play chess, these machines can win the game against a human opponent, self-driving cars have mastered the ability to absorb all the external data surrounding them and compute it fast enough that they can navigate and reach their destination without causing an accident of some kind. Smart homes can interact with members of the household, control the temperature, manage security, and even food supply to ensure the comfort of its inhabitants.

Of course, when anything completely new is introduced to the world, there is often some skepticism involved and the same could be true in regards to artificial intelligence. Even though we interact with AI on a daily basis, most of us don't realize it. Whenever you talk to SIRI through an Apple device, you're using artificial intelligence. Alexa from Amazon also makes use of the same technology. These devices, though impressive, are considered to be what is called 'narrow AI' or a 'weak AI.' They are only programmed to perform a very small number of tasks. These merely represent the first introductory steps of AI on a long-term goal towards a more human interaction with machines. With that said, aside from the fears that many people have about AI, there are numerous benefits that we will gain from these advantages.

Artificial intelligence in medicine

When it comes to healthcare, artificial intelligence is already making impressive progress, especially in the field of health. While we have not reached the point of developing a strong AI, artificial intelligence is already a major part of our lives. With a machine capable of thinking and reasoning, treatment of patients will be much more efficient. Physicians will have easy access to all the data they need and these machines will be instrumental in helping them make a good decision.

This type of technology won't be available until sometime far into the future. Currently, many people are creating algorithms that will help them solve many of the problems in healthcare today. We're not looking at 100 or 200 years down the road but more like five to ten years.

Right now, IBM's Watson is leading the pack with its cognitive computing used for healthcare. They are closely followed by neural networks developed by big names such as Dell, Hewlett-Packard, Apple, Hitachi, Digital Reasoning, Sentient Technologies, and more.

With each new advancement made by these companies, health care improves by a greater margin. Right now, there are countless areas in the field of medicine being addressed. We will see progress in the following areas:

- **Data management**

  AI will be primarily responsible for collecting it, storing, it, analyzing it, and drawing conclusions from it. For example, the Google Deepmind Health project is already mining medical records in order to come up with a way to provide better health services for patients. For now, they are working with the Moorfield Eye Hospital NHS Foundation on ways to improve eye treatment.

- IBM's Watson mentioned earlier that its artificial intelligence is working with oncologists to improve the way of analyzing evidence-based treatment options. It has already improved the ability to analyze the meaning and the context of data found in clinical notes and reports. This information, once difficult to decipher, could be very instrumental in finding a workable treatment by combining multiple aspects from a patient's file with external research to identify the best course of treatment. The belief is that one day, Watson may be the best resource for patients struggling with cancer. Watson impressed many by analyzing 3,500 medical textbooks and 400,000 other pieces of related data, all in 17 seconds, to come up with a viable treatment option for the patient. It is expected that Watson will be rolled out to the mainstream population by the end of 2018.

- Another artificial intelligence from IBM is the Medical Sieve. This is an exploratory project that is labeled as a 'cognitive assistant.' This AI analyzes, and reasons on a vast amount of clinical data that is then used in the decision-making process in fields of radiology and cardiology. It can analyze radiology images and identify anomalies that point out health problems much faster than the human eye. In the future, radiologists will only need to view the most complicated of cases where human supervision will be necessary.

- Genetics study will also benefit greatly from artificial intelligence. The Deep Genomics project is at work identifying patterns in a massive compilation of genetic information and medical records. The project is looking for mutations and other anomalies that could help detect diseases very early on. Their work on inventing a whole new generation of computers that will let doctors see what happens inside a cell once the DNA is altered by its genes.

- The Human Genome project is busy developing an algorithm that could make it possible to spot cancer and vascular diseases in the early stages.

- Artificial intelligence will also help in developing pharmaceuticals through clinical trials, which normally take years to develop. By getting through this process many times faster, billions of dollars will be saved and more people will receive treatment for less money.

These are only a few of the examples of artificial intelligence at work today in the healthcare industry. With so much data flooding into the system, it is virtually impossible for humans to sift through it all. Consider the sheer number of patient medical records, treatment data, and all of the other technological devices that are accumulating information about health. All of this could be analyzed in a matter of seconds where it would take humans years to digest it. This means that healthcare will naturally improve and more people will be able to receive faster and better treatment than they have ever had before.

Artificial intelligence in finance

Another area where artificial intelligence is already making an impression is in the finance industry. As of now, nearly every financial company in the industry is ready to embrace AI. It not only will save them time, it will cut costs, and add value to their services.

A perfect example of this is the AI computer Wealthfront, which tracks user account activity in order to analyze account holder's spending behavior. By understanding this behavior, the company can help them make proper financial decisions and even customize the advice they give to their clients.

As of 2016, more than 550 financial companies have already started using artificial intelligence in their business, generating an additional $5 billion in revenue. In fact, the top seven US commercial banks also are making AI a priority as a means of servicing their customer base better. As a result, they were able to improve performance and generate more income at the same time.

Consider the results generated by JPMorgan Chase's 'Contract Intelligence' platform, which uses AI image recognition software to extract important data from legal documents. Normally, this task would take approximately 360,000 hours of manpower while the AI did it all in a matter of seconds.

Finance is expected to be heavily influenced by artificial intelligence in every aspect. It is already setting the stage for a complete renovation among the industry leaders, making them more competitive in the process. Any company that has not tapped into artificial intelligence will quickly find themselves falling behind in their ability to maximize their resources, lower their risks, increase their revenue streams, increase their ability to trade, invest, lend, and more.

All of this is now being done through automation. Many of the once repetitive tasks are now being handled through neural networks in artificial intelligence. Their software is capable of matching data records, analyzing and looking for exceptions, and placing the decision-making process in the hand of this new technology. Since AI is designed to be a learning machine that will be constantly improving itself, in time they will be able to take over more of the mundane and repetitive jobs that are now consuming many hours of manpower.

Right now, AI in the finance industry is primarily used in three areas:

- Calculating parameters and numbers beyond human capabilities

- Analyzing and interpreting written text by using a special program that allows them to grasp the context of the language used in contracts and agreements

- Pattern recognition to detect different types of activity, audit books, and inspect finances in ways that go beyond human accuracy

The benefits of AI in the finance industry will be better trading by making selections through algorithms, better investment insights, improved risk management, improved fraud detection, and better choices when it comes to making credit decisions.

There are countless applications that are already being put to good use in financial services, and there is more of that to come in the future. So, the next time you need to make an investment decision or receive a recommendation from your financial institution, it's a good bet that you're getting your advice from some form of artificial intelligence.

Artificial intelligence in translation

Today, there are more than 6,000 languages spoken around the globe. Anytime someone needs to communicate with someone from another language group problems arise. In most cases, if one party does not understand the other, there will be a need for a translator. This is not only time consuming but expensive.

Now though, according to two separate research papers, artificial intelligence is beginning to become a major part of the translation industry. There are now several different AI programs that use unsupervised artificial intelligence that can perform language translation efficiently without the use of a language dictionary. The methods work both with parallel text as well as with identical text that is already being used in other languages.

These programs begin with data specifically chosen to supply them with an extensive bilingual dictionary that they can reference without the aid of a human to verify their answers. The machines rely on the relationship that exists between words. For example, tree and leaves or shoes and socks. These relationships exist in some form in all languages. The AI looks at these words and groups them into clusters and connects them from one language to another to help them understand how the syntax of another language is formed.

The dictionary the computer builds from the data is then put together with two additional AI methods called 'back translation' and 'denoising.' Back translation translates one sentence into the new language and then translates it back again as a way of testing its accuracy. If the back-translated sentence doesn't match the original, the system will automatically readjust its parameters and make a second attempt. It will continue to do this until it gets as close as possible to the correct answer. Denoising works in a similar way but goes an additional step. It randomly removes a word from the sentence to make sure that the AI is also building on the structure of the sentence rather than just translating them word for word.

Google and Facebook both have incorporated language translation into their platform successfully. We can fully expect more artificial intelligence applications in language translation to be introduced in the future.

There is no doubt that machine translation has improved a great deal in recent years. It is much more accurate, it works at impressive speeds, and it is readily available in almost every language you speak.

A good example of this is Google translate. According to their records, the machine translator has an impressive accuracy that is on par with human translators. Every day, it translates Spanish, Chinese, French, as well as many other languages to English and back again both accurately and quickly. As their program continues to learn, it has reached high accuracy levels so it can be relied on in a wide range of business applications. Today, machine translation is being used in government, software and technology, military and defense, healthcare, finance, legal, and E-commerce.

Whether the need is for text to text, text to speech, speech to text, speech to speech, or even an image to text, there is an AI program that can handle it.

Game playing

While the other applications of artificial intelligence deal with the serious matters of business, money, and health, there is another area where these programs have made a lasting impression that is not always so serious. This is not to say that game playing is not as important as the other industries. In fact, for many, the art of game playing is, in reality, a very serious business.

It would actually be a miscarriage of justice to ignore the gaming industry when talking about modern technology. For many decades now, board games have been at the center of AI research, in more recent years we've witnessed the progression widen out to incorporate video games as well. In fact, video games have become even more sophisticated in many ways mainly because of the introduction of artificial intelligence.

These programs are designed to control non-player characters, generating data about their opponents and adapting to their behaviors. Game developers have realized that using AI programs to analyze large amounts of data generated from players from all over the globe has helped them develop games that are more intricately designed.

While gamers are a small community in comparison with the other major industries, it is growing in popularity mainly because of what they have learned by applying artificial intelligence analysis in their designs.

It is a thriving field of research, but it is also a phenomenal playing field for testing out new algorithms that can one day be adopted into other industries as well. In fact, it is with the gaming industry that AI often introduces new programs that have gone on to increase computational power and generate countless stories of success in many other industries.

Think about some of the common uses for AI today that was actually started and tested first in the gaming world.

- Image and speech recognition
- Emotion detection
- Self-driving cars
- Web searching
- Creative design

All of these concepts that are now part of the real world were first tested in a game of some kind.

All this helps us see just how important the gaming world is to modern technology. Just like many scientific ideas were first introduced to the world through science fiction books, TV shows, and movies, much of the technology that makes them possible was introduced through games.

But what about game playing itself? The fact is, the gaming world is the safest environment where scientific problem solving can work in harmony with creativity. AI helps humans to better understand how we play games, how we understand the interactions between players, and therefore how to build a better game.

But gaming AI is not limited to the board games or even the online versions of many games but is playing a major role in the gaming industry. You know the kind of games that go in Las Vegas, Reno, and Atlantic City? Once upon a time, these were the only locations where one could put money down on a poker game or gamble a little on the turn of a roulette wheel. But because of artificial intelligence, these games can now be played with just as much vigor as you would if you were there in person. Now, poker games are popping up all over the world. You might be sitting across the table with one player in Japan, another in Spain, and another in South Africa.

These types of games have become profitable ventures on all fronts. Many people who would have previously been unknown have become world-renowned players for their winning streaks.

New games have also begun to emerge as a result of artificial intelligence. The game Nevermind, introduced in 2016 is capable of tracking how a player's emotions unfold during the game and adjust its playing strategy accordingly.

Games have been a prominent area for testing AI and will continue to be so. Not only does it provide programmers a safe place to test new algorithms and designs, it is also the one place where there can be true human-computer interactions so we can see how it plays out in the future. The simple fact that games are so popular opens the door to amazing possibilities. People are more willing to test them out, computers have a wealth of data to analyze, and they can create a host of problems and challenges that can be worked out over time.

Chapter 7:
Neural Networks in the Future

I t's hard to imagine the possibilities the future holds for neural networks. Because of how this technology is already 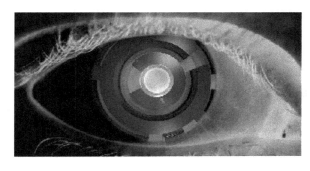 integrating themselves into every aspect of our lives, the potential for new and innovative ideas is higher than ever. We can envision a Jetson-like world where we will have self-driving cars instead of GPS devices that need to be programmed with our intended destination. Imagine a car that has learned your personal preferences in the music you listen to, the temperature you're most comfortable with, and how to perfectly adjust your seat.

But all of that is possible now. The future holds a lot more possibilities where neural networks can be applied.

There are two different ways that this new learning technology can grow. One area is in the field of virtual intelligence. This type of program could be planned, controlled, predictable, and could eventually become the next evolutionary step in artificial intelligence.

This type of intelligence would be even closer to matching its thinking and learning styles to humans. A machine that can evolve and grow with mankind, adapt to the same environment and learn from its experiences is inevitable.

To advance to this point, however, requires technology that can actually understand and make the necessary adjustments to bridge the gap that now exists between AI and VI. As this new technology slowly engages in our world, more of our activities will be played out in virtual reality. We'll find ourselves spending more time with computers, giving the loads of data to share. We'll communicate through the use of avatars, social platforms, and games.

These virtual worlds will have to be created though, but these are places where it is safe to learn, try, and fail at our attempts to improve. They will take the place of social platforms and make it possible for us to hone our skills in business, finance, and even romance. Whatever you want to test out, there will be a virtual world to work in before you make your idea mainstream.

This will eventually become a fully automated world but not a self-aware world as many people fear. Humans will still set the parameters and put limits on the kind of things they want computers to do. Their intelligent software will be able to simplify and enhance our real life but not take charge and control it. As long as humans put limits on the computer's ability to grow, the future will remain bright for this technological advancement.

Right now, artificial intelligence is still in its infancy, the next decade could be a real eye-opener. Not very far in the future, we will begin to see these machines change the way cars and planes are designed, how they will be operated, and how they will interact with humans. We will watch our days of exploration go further and further into space. In time, we will witness the colonization of new worlds. This time literally.

The future also has many changes in store for a country's military might. Soon, there won't be a need for "boots on the ground" when a country is at war. One soldier will be able to manage an entire fleet of drones that will fight in their place. These are already in use in some partial form now. Called unmanned aerial vehicles or UAVs these drones are capable of being operated from a remote location and responding to a myriad of instructions. In time, these UAVs will become autonomous and work without the aid of human direction.

What does this mean? Imagine a fleet of drones all headed for a single target. If one drone is destroyed by enemy fire, the remaining drones could automatically reassemble and continue on to accomplish their mission. Their ability to learn and grow will allow them to adapt to the function of the destroyed drone and incorporate his assigned task into their programming.

It is expected that with each new system introduced, machine programming will increase in its complexity and capabilities. Today, we think that artificial intelligence is one of the most fascinating forms of technology known to man. What will we think when virtual intelligence becomes available to the mainstream population? These machines will be more capable of interacting with humans and will revolutionize every aspect of our daily life.

Another area where this new technology will improve human life is in the field of disaster response. Areas unsafe for humans to enter can now be accessed by deploying machines to bring aid to people who are cut off from the rest of the world by catastrophic events. Imagine how these intelligent programs can be installed in machines that can search for life underneath the rubble of ruined buildings. How food supplies can be delivered quickly and safely. How rebuilding efforts will be much faster and how the treatment of the injured will be done quickly and efficiently.

We'll see this technology in the movie industry, music, in agriculture, and in an endless parade of other industries as time progresses. Right now, we are pretty sure of what the future holds for a neural network and all of its many applications. What we are not sure of is how quickly humankind will embrace it. No doubt, it will be the younger and more adventurous generation that will embrace it first. They will be the ones to harness its immense potential and they will be the ones who will have to set its limits.

Science has a lot to offer us in the way of advanced computer technology. The machines which will be produced tomorrow and in the years to come will open the door to a whole new world of adventure. But it will happen because people are driven by the powerful force of human desire to always find better ways to do things are stronger than the many who are powerful and in time, they will make the science fiction of the past become the reality of today.

Conclusion

There is no doubt that we have entered into a whole new era in mankind's industry. Perhaps in the very near future, we will have other artificial intelligence with which we can communicate, to share our ideals and thoughts with. While that time may be far off in the future, it is beginning today. With the aid of neural networks, we now have the power to change the world in many ways.

Neural networks are the very key to the future. No matter what your goals are, what you expect out of life, or what you plan to do, soon, nearly every computer on the planet will be equipped with some sort of neural network. Businesses are using it to improve customer service as well as boost their bottom line. Governments are using it to plan future cities and to better understand the ones we live in today. Other industries are utilizing it to help improve their bottom line, and private citizens also find that even they have a reason to take a closer look at this new and innovative technology. In this book, you've learned a great deal about neural networks.

No matter where you stand, you need to realize that these tiny little machines are going to change your life forever. With the help of this book, you have learned a lot. By now, you should understand what neural networks are and the many algorithms and other components that make it possible for a machine to learn.

You've learned that neural networks are the key component that allows the machine to learn. Without them, the network is simply reduced down to a very basic and simple vending machine that takes in information and then gives you what you want.

But neural networks are far from using such a simple strategy. You also learned the main concepts behind neural networks, the basic architecture, some of the rules and guidelines that have been set to help the machine to learn. You learned about the technical fields and how they operate, and the many different ways that neural networks can be applied in our day-to-day lives.

No doubt, this book has probably raised more questions than answers but it is our hope that we have at least piqued your interest so that you are eager to learn more. There is much to learn on this subject and sad to say, we have barely just scratched the surface.

Regardless of what you expect to achieve with this knowledge, you have taken the first step in your quest to better understand neural networks and their role in our lives today, tomorrow, and well on into the future.

Finally, if you found this book useful in any way, a review on Amazon is always appreciated!

Deep Learning
Step-by-Step

A Sensible Guide Presenting the Concepts of
Deep Learning with Real World Examples

Matthew Harper

for any hardship or damages that may befall them after undertaking information described herein.

Additionally, the information in the following pages is intended only for informational purposes and should thus be thought of as universal. As befitting its nature, it is presented without assurance regarding its prolonged validity or interim quality. Trademarks that are mentioned are done without written consent and can in no way be considered an endorsement from the trademark holder.

Table of Contents

Introduction

Congratulations on downloading *Deep Learning Step-by-Step* and thank you for doing so.

If you are new to the concept of deep learning, you might assume that it is some fundamental of education, a better way to teach in the classroom. Something along the lines of a new and innovative way to get students to absorb more information. If you have some foundation in computer science, then you would have a general idea of what it really is. While you would be wrong on the first assumption, you would still be close to grasping the basic idea of deep learning. However, there is one fundamental difference that makes it unique.

Deep learning is not about people, but instead, a method of machine learning. Yes, the machines are actually the students in this concept. It is a learning system that uses algorithms that have been developed that attempts to mimic the human brain and the way it gathers information, analyzes, and makes decisions based on the data received. In essence, through the use of these algorithms, deep learning makes it possible for machines to absorb new information and to apply it to their functions.

It helps to understand a little about the human brain functions to help us see how deep learning actually works. For thousands of years, the human brain has been the hallmark of intelligent life. No other creature on the planet has come close to having the capacity of the human brain. Its ability to capture millions of bits of information through its senses, process it, reason on it, store information, and dictate to the body exactly how it should respond has mystified scientists for eons. For the layperson, it can be quite difficult to see exactly how machine learning could possibly have the ability to do the same thing.

There are quite a few similarities that machines now have in common with the human brain as well as differences. Understanding the way learning happens naturally can help us to understand how a machine can be programmed to learn in this phenomenal new type of technology.

In the human brain, learning stems from its millions of interconnected neurons. These could be likened to the tiny connections you might find in a spider web but with an amazing difference. When the brain is exposed to some form of stimulation, these neurons instinctively adjust to the new information by changing their configuration. With each change, new connections are formed, old ones are strengthened, and those that have not been used for a long time are eliminated. This is why the more one completes a task, the better they get at it.

Think about this, if you are learning to play the piano, the first time you touch the keys your performance will be clumsy and awkward. You are unsure of where the keys are, which ones to hit, and how long to hold each note, and how the note will harmonize with the one before it or after it. But if you make it a habit to practice regularly, you'll find that you will eventually approach the keyboard and play songs, notes, and tunes without even thinking about it. The neurons that fired when you were practicing will have become very strong from repeated use.

If you continue to practice, eventually you could become a master pianist.

Our neurons are capable of processing all sorts of stimuli by utilizing tools from our memory and our perceptions at the time. Each time it receives stimuli through our five senses, a different subset of our enormous supply of neurons is triggered creating knowledge.

Neuroscience (or the study of the brain) is the biological pattern from which deep learning has been created. The networks that process deep learning have been labeled as "artificial neural networks" or ANN because they are designed to mimic the same neural pathways of the human brain. While a neural network cannot exactly replicate the amazing ability of the human brain, the general concept is very similar. Throughout the pages of this book, we will break down the complex design of these artificial neural networks (ANN) so you can better grasp what deep learning is and the myriad of ways it can be used.

Chapter 1:
A Brief Overview of Deep Learning

D eep learning has probably become one of the most complex developments that mankind has created to date. Scientists have gone far beyond creating machines that can learn, making the technology we have now seem like ancient history before we even have the chance to fully grasp it.

Why Do We Need it?

There are millions of different uses for deep learning, most of them probably haven't been thought of yet but its practical applications even today have already proved to be revolutionary in their ability to simplify our world around us.

No doubt, for the average person, the idea can be extremely intimidating, but reality tells us that its implementation in our daily lives will only continue to grow. It is already being used in space for special projects like the Google Brain, and DeepMind. It is the technology that anticipates what movies you will watch next on Netflix, which is the same technology that determines what advertisements flash before your eyes when you're searching the Internet.

The fact is that deep learning is one of the few methods that allow us to get around many challenges. It makes it possible to have a machine focus on certain elements in a situation or environment without being programmed to do so. Still, it is very easy to see how machine learning is needed today. Even now, machines that can do deep learning are able to master certain skills that before only humans could do.

For example, these machines can recognize patterns. They can decipher facial identities and facial expressions. This can help in protecting us from identity theft and a host of other criminal activities. They can even identify speech patterns so that the way we speak can be used to identify us, the same way our fingerprints or DNA are already used. The benefits of this alone are phenomenal.

Deep learning also helps machines to recognize various anomalies. Financial institutions are already using them to identify unusual sequences that are out of the norm when purchases or made. Nuclear power plants use them to monitor sensor readings, so they can determine the potential for a critical event long before it becomes a danger.

Deep learning can be used in making more accurate predictions, so we can better plan for the future. Whether it is weather changes or fluctuations in stock prices, knowing what is more likely to happen tomorrow, next month or next year are important factors that can help us make many important decisions in our life; this ability can find practical uses in all sorts of industries. Imagine what can be done in genetics, in health, in science, in manufacturing, and in a host of other fields we all rely on.

While machines are still a long way from matching perfectly the tasks that the human brain can do, the use of deep learning can definitely usher us into a whole new way of learning that goes beyond the simplistic abilities they have had in the past. Only time will tell what deep learning will provide us within the coming years.

History of Deep Learning

A mere five years ago, the concept of deep learning was mostly relegated to be a niche field of interest. It was far from a programming method adopted by the mainstream population. But in that very short period of time, there has been a marked increase in this type of machine learning. If you've been connected in the computer science fields for any length of time, you've probably already noticed that research on the subject has been repeatedly recorded in computer journals like Science Nature, JAMA, and Nature Methods. Even if you're not in the field of science, you've no doubt heard about the Smart Cars that can drive themselves, the computer that was able to copy a masterpiece painting, or even their ability to diagnose major health diseases.

Even with all the hype and excitement around it today, it is interesting to note that the main idea behind deep learning has been in place for decades. However, this global fascination with the machine learning couldn't fully materialize until computers had the ability to work at speeds fast enough to make it possible to tap into the true power behind it. There have been several milestones that have been instrumental in putting deep learning on the global scientific map, let's take a look at some of them.

Early in the 1940s, during the heart of World War II, the concept of a thinking machine was first introduced. It was first mentioned in a seminal paper by Alan Turing, *Computing*

Machinery and Intelligence. In his paper, Turing points out several very specific criteria that would determine whether or not it was even possible for a computer to be intelligent. The criteria eventually became known as the 'Turing test.'

- **Electronic Brain – 1943**

  In those days, machine learning was limited because our understanding of the human brain was far from accurate. The first to work on the concept of an electronic brain were two scientists by the names of Walter Pitts and Warren McCulloch who developed a technique called the "threshold logic unit," which was designed to mimic the way people thought a neuron worked in a real brain. It was dubbed "the electronic brain."

- **Perceptron – 1957**

  This idea had its limits since an accurate understanding of how the brain worked had yet to be discovered. The concept of a thinking machine was stalled until Frank Rosenblatt introduced a program called, "Perceptron" in 1957. This turned out to be the precursor for the modern neural networks we use today. Perceptron, for its time, was an amazing discovery. Considered to be the "embryo of an electronic computer," it was expected to allow machines to be able to walk, talk, see, and write in pretty much the same way as humans would. It gave machines the ability to recognize and identify letters and numbers and was believed that in time, a machine programmed with perceptron would be able to reproduce and be aware of its own existence. This was the first time we were to hear the words "Artificial Intelligence."

Perceptron had its own limitations though. As it began to generate growing interest in the scientific community, those limitations became very evident. As they noticed, these machines could differentiate between numbers and letters, the results were not consistent. It could recognize an E from an F or a 5 from a 6, but if other stimuli were found near or around the figures it was trying to read, the machine's ability to identify what it was seeing literally fell apart. The problem became known as the XOr Problem.

The conclusion that resulted was that many determined it to be impossible for a machine to learn regardless of how much time was invested in training it. This belief virtually put the idea of perceptron as the birth of the neural net on hold indefinitely.

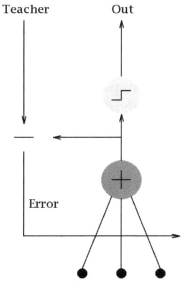

- **ADALINE/MADELINE – 1960**

Soon after, ADALINE was introduced by Bernard Widrow. Similar to perceptron, it used a threshold logic device designed to perform a linear summation of inputs and then classify them into different patterns. The algorithm used for Adaline was a learning control mechanism that took various input data, analyzed it and made comparisons before generating specific outputs.

Adaline had a 5-step learning procedure:

- o Set all weights and thresholds to small bipolar random values

- o Introduce new inputs along with the desired outputs

- o Calculate the actual outputs

- o Adapt the weights

- o Repeat steps two to four until the desired outputs and the actual outputs are equal

While Adaline had the same basic neural structure as Perceptron had, it was found that it could only distinguish linearly separable patterns. This made it one step closer to future artificial intelligence, but it was still short of the ultimate goal.

Another system created about the same time was MADELINE, which used numerous adaptive linear neurons, but they were arranged in a multilayer network. This type of program used a majority vote rule on the outputs from the Adaline layer. In other words, if more than 50% of the outputs from Adaline were a +1 then the Madeline would also have an output of +1. This gave Madeline the ability to classify nonlinear functions that were similar to multi-layer Perceptron.

Madeline had a six-step learning procedure:

- o Initialize weights and thresholds

- o   Present new inputs and desired outputs

- o   Calculate the actual outputs

- o   Determine the actual Madeline outputs

- o   Determine error and update weights

- o   Repeat steps two to five until the desired outputs and the actual outputs are equal for all vectors

- **Addressing the XOr Problem – 1969**

In time, perceptron began to attract a lot of attention again, especially by Marvin Minsky, who would later become the father of artificial intelligence. While on the surface the concept seemed good, Minsky was the one who detected problems with the program. His concern lied not in what the machine was able to do but instead of what it couldn't. While the machine could learn, it was incapable of learning the exclusive function or the XOr. Minsky also proved that not only could the machine NOT learn this function but that it was theoretically impossible to learn it.

To solve the problems, he proposed a new structure of the pattern of neural networks with a special output labeled as the "Reject output". This was meant to be used to separate out any patterns that the machine would have difficulty recognizing.

- **Multi-Layered Perceptron or Backpropagation – 1986**

It took years for interest to build up again in the field. It wasn't until the 1980s that another spark of life began to emerge. A new individual entered the arena by the name of Geoff Hinton. He along with David Rumelhart and Ronald Williams published a paper, *"Learning representation by back-propagating errors."* Here they explained that it was possible for the numerous hidden layers of neural nets to be trained. The procedure was relatively simple; by using these hidden layers it was possible for these nets to bypass the weakness of perceptron. It appeared that they now had figured out a way to give the network the ability to learn nonlinear functions. In fact, it was also discovered that these networks could learn any function with these hidden layers.

The algorithm was able to work by using the derivative of the networks' loss function and back-propagating the errors in order to update the parameters of the lower layers. The first attempts to try this algorithm were quite successful especially when it trained convolutional neural nets to recognize handwritten digits.

However, as successful as it was in the early stages, their efforts were not able to yield the same results with larger problems, sending the concept into another deep freeze where research was all but stopped once again.

- **SVM – 1995**

A decade later, the 90s introduced the Support Vector Machine (SVM). This quickly became the preferred method of machine learning, which quickly sent the neural nets to the back of the line. It would be another decade and a half before they were able to be brought out again. The problem then was that their computing power was much too slow to do what they were attempting to do.

- **Deep Neural Network – 2006**

  Around 2006, Hinton announced that he finally knew how the human brain really worked and introduced a new idea. The unsupervised pre-training and deep belief nets became the next advancement in machine learning. The concept was to train a restricted Boltzmann machine, an unsupervised model, to freeze all parameters. Then they would add a new layer over them and train only the parameters of the new layer. In that vein, they could continue adding and training layers until you had built up a deep network. Finally, they would use the result to initialize the parameters of the traditional neural network. With this strategy, they found it was possible to train networks that were much deeper than any other attempts they had previously made.

- **Breakthrough – 2012**

  Now that interest was building up again, more people dove into the research. 2012 was the year that things literally began to take off for deep learning. They had begun to use these deep nets for speech recognition. It was the first time that a neural model had been able to be considered "state of the art."

However, more complications were in the future. As these neural nets began to surpass the more traditional methods used, things did not always pan out as they expected. The issue was addressed head-on in 2012 at the Large Scale Visual Recognition Challenge. This was a competition where challengers could build their own computer vision models, submit predictions, and be scored according to their accuracy. The first two years of the competition (2010, 2011), the top winners had error rates of 26 and 28%. However, in 2012, Geoff Hinton along with Alex Krizhevsky, and Ilya Sutskever submitted a model that yielded an error rate of only 16% literally blowing the competition out of the water.

How were they able to accomplish this? They used graphics processing units (GPUs) in their training approach. Because GPUs are basically parallel floating-point calculators with hundreds or thousands of cores, they were able to operate must faster allowing them to train larger models. This made it possible for them to achieve much lower error rates. In addition, they were able to introduce something called a dropout, which allowed them to lower their overfitting and use the rectified linear activation unit. Both of these became their main components for modern-day deep learning. Their network became known as Alexnet.

Alexnet ushered in a whole new era. After its introduction, many more new innovations have been introduced in rapid succession. It was the machine that finally gave deep learning its wings. Today, it is believed that we are on the very precipice of a full-scale artificial intelligence age. Nearly every industry in existence is shelling out billions of dollars on research and to acquire AI technology and the talent to run it. Right now, we are in a paradigm shift in machine learning and there is no turning back.

Chapter 2:
What You Need to Know to Get Started with Deep Learning

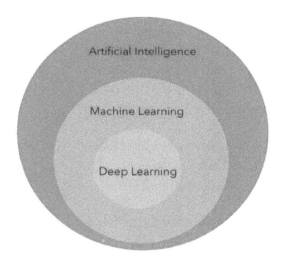

The innovations and breakthroughs that have been accomplished with deep learning are enough to get a lot of people excited about it. It is said that we live in the age of technology and with the many strides already achieved by deep learning, the next age will probably be the age of artificial intelligence. To that end, there will be more and more people looking to enter this field, so they can have a role in ushering in this new era.

However, before they can do that there are a lot of things you must come to understand. Now that these fundamentals are so clearly realized, we will begin to see artificial intelligence emerge in all sorts of industries. We've already discussed how it is being used in areas of pattern recognition, and object detection, but the extent of deep learning will one day go much further than that.

This is a complex field and for anyone to get a firm grasp on it, it helps to have a basic understanding of subjects like linear algebra, calculus, probability, and programming. This knowledge will be very beneficial in helping you to grasp the concepts we will be mentioning later in this book. If you don't have this background, it doesn't mean that you cannot grasp these concepts, but it does mean you'll have to do a little extra homework to get through the meat of it all.

You'll also need to know some practical differences in how deep learning differs and why it is so much more efficient than any other type of artificial intelligence before it.

Deep Learning, Machine Learning, Artificial Intelligence – What's the Difference?

Often when you research deep learning you'll come across several different terms that seem to be used interchangeably. Deep learning, machine learning, and artificial intelligence. While these are all related there are some distinct differences that set them all apart from each other.

So, what exactly is deep learning? Basically, it is a type of machine learning that uses a system of neural networks that are designed to mimic the learning of the human brain. This network's focus is to simplify how a machine uses certain learning algorithms, which can be applied in artificial intelligence and machine learning. In fact, it is virtually impossible to have artificial intelligence without deep learning.

Because of deep learning, we now have the ability to develop massively large neural networks that have the ability to absorb information and respond to it without the need for a human to program it's every move. The expectation is that one day, these machines will be able to operate autonomously, completely on their own without any form of human interference.

For the layperson, we are familiar with the term "artificial intelligence." It is the stuff of countless science fiction movies. However, few people understand that it is no longer science fiction but is definitely emerging in the realm of reality.

To explain:

- Deep learning is a form of machine learning that is used to teach machines how to learn in a way that is similar to the learning process in the human brain.

- Machine learning is a series of algorithms that give machines the ability to collect data, analyze it, and make decisions based on that analysis.

- Artificial intelligence is a machine programmed with machine learning, so it can gather data and make decisions based on that data.

In its most basic of forms, deep learning is simply another type of machine learning. Basic machine learning has improved over the years and deep learning is the latest link in the evolutionary chain. In its early stages of development, deep learning machines were only capable of learning from data that had already been labeled and stored into the machine. This meant it could only function with human supervision. Unsupervised learning was still far into the future, but many believed it was a very real possibility. Now, machines can learn in all sorts of ways.

How a Machine Learns

When it comes to learning, we humans do it without any thinking or programming. Our minds have never had to be trained in how to learn something. From the time we're born, our five senses go immediately into action, collecting data and submitting it to our brains. Our brains process it, analyze it, and then make decisions based on it. If we're walking out at night, our brain automatically assesses the scene, determines a level of danger, and tells our feet to move faster. If we're watching a movie, our brain takes all that information in and determines whether we should cry, laugh, or be angry. We have what is called unsupervised learning. No one has to program those details and responses into us.

In addition, once we learn a concept, it then becomes a foundation from which we can build on. We first learn the alphabet (the initial concept) then we learn the sounds related to that alphabet, then we learn to string sounds together, creating words. Eventually, we'll be able to read and this is called layered learning. With that thought in mind, we can continue to build our knowledge base and grow from there.

The concept behind machine learning is similar. While it is a far cry from doing the amazing things that a human brain can do, its function is based on a similar set of situations. A massive set of neural networks are created, each one communicating with the other. It also collects data and responds to the information it receives.

With artificial intelligence, the machine will be able to take in raw data and respond with a selection of pre-programmed responses. They will be able to "learn" from the data input and build on it. The major difference is that at present, machines can only learn from human input and develop their own concepts from the information gathered. This is one step closer to mimicking the human learning process.

Deep learning is basically a unique form of machine learning that is much more flexible than other previous forms used. By using a nested hierarchy of concepts, it can access many layers of non-linear information processing and achieve both supervised and unsupervised learning, which is ideal for pattern analysis and classification.

Deep neural networks consist of several layers called a hierarchical neural network. In this type of network, every layer has the ability to change its input data into something that is more abstract. The output layer will then combine the various features of input data and formulate a prediction. This method improves calculations, so it is much easier to understand.

While there are several different ways that machines can learn information, their strategies can be categorized into two separate classes. The first being supervised learning that uses labeled data to classify information. This form of learning is based on data that produces "expected answers." For example:

- Visual Recognition

  Imagine an AI designed to identify pedestrians walking across a street. It can be trained by inputting millions of short videos of street scenes collected. Some of the videos will have pedestrians walking while other videos will not. Some of the videos will have many people walking while some may have only one.

  With a number of learning algorithms applied to the data, each giving the machine access to the correct answers a variety of models are designed to teach the machine how to identify pedestrians in fast-moving scenes. The algorithms are tested against an unlabeled set of data that will check for accuracy.

- Predictions

  Supervised learning can also be used in making different predictions. A machine can be taught to estimate risk by inputting a large number of actual trades made by real investors and the results they received. It can then be asked to give an estimate of risk for each trade based on several fundamental factors of previous trades: price, volume, company, etc.

  It then takes its estimated risk and compares it to the historical results during several different time intervals (day, week, month, and year) to determine if its predictions are accurate or within normal expectations.

Unsupervised learning works a little differently. The machine receives input without any related yield factors. The answers are derived purely from the calculations made. The goal of this type of learning is to demonstrate the basic structure or dissemination of the information so that the machine can gather even more details about the information. Unlike with supervised learning, the machine is not given any right answer and there is no human instructor guiding its data. The AI may collect the data and sort it according to its similarities or differences even if there is no classification. The goal is to show a fundamental structure in the information in an effort to get a better understanding of it.

It is referred to as unsupervised learning because there is no instructor guiding it to the right conclusions. The machine will perform its own calculations in an effort to determine the nature of the data that it has collected.

While there are obvious advantages to unsupervised learning, there are still some problems it has yet to resolve. For example, a machine may be capable of identifying basic visual images (it can tell a cat from a dog) it may also end up creating new classifications in an attempt to distinguish between varying differences within a certain classification. (It may not be able to tell a German shepherd from a Chihuahua). Its purpose is to find relationships within the data it receives but this can create several problems when it tries to go further than that.

Clustering is when the AI attempts to decipher different groups within the data whereas association is an attempt to determine specific rules that will describe the data. Both of these can present huge problems in AI when their results are skewed by unanticipated groupings.

In reinforcement learning, the machine is trained to recognize activities. To come to this conclusion, it learns from its own actions and not from a human instructor giving it the necessary input. The goal, in this case, is not to make a classification or a prediction of events but instead to develop a policy of behavior.

We can find a perfect example of this in our relationship with household pets. If you're going to teach your dog a new trick, you can't just input the information and give it instructions on how you want it to behave. However, if you reward it for doing something and penalize it for other actions, eventually the dog will learn how to do the things that give it rewards and avoid the behavior and those actions that bring on discipline.

Reinforcement learning in machines works in a similar way with a few differences.

- Substitute the pet with the machine

- Substitute the treat for a reward function

- Substitute the good behavior with a resultant action

In order for this to work, you need to have a feedback loop that will reinforce what the machine is actually learning. It is rewarded when it performs certain actions and is disciplined when it is wrong. You might wonder how you can reward or discipline a machine that has no feelings and no emotions. The system will work something like this:

- The machine is given an internal state that it must maintain. This state is used to learn about their environment.

- The reward function is used to teach the machine how to behave.

- The environment is the situation or scenario that the machine must operate in. It consists of all the things the agent can observe and respond to.

- The action is the behavior of the machine.

- The agent performs all the deeds.

Let's apply this to the computer game, Mario. As the machine attempts to play the game it has an environment that allows it to perform many different functions. It does not know what will happen when it performs each of these functions. It can't see the entire environment at a single time, so it must navigate through the environment and make decisions on what to do. If it makes a move that will not advance it, then it is "punished" by not allowing it to move further. If it makes a move that advances it through the environment, it is "rewarded." In time the machine will learn exactly how to navigate safely through its environment until it reaches the conclusion of the game.

This is a very basic explanation of reinforcement learning but it should be enough to give you a general idea of how it works in machine learning. This form of unsupervised learning is not completely without human input. Someone has to create the environment that the machine will operate in as well as the consequences of each move. However, many are looking at this type of machine learning as the true future of artificial intelligence.

There are many applications and uses for machine learning and deep learning by extension that go far beyond the obvious. Already these learning mechanisms are being used in anomaly detection, human genome projects, sequencing analysis, crime analysis, and climatology among countless other uses and no doubt, there will be more practical applications that will be discovered in the future.

Chapter 3:
Understanding Neural Networks

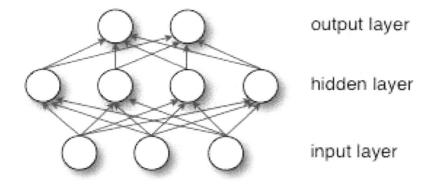

As we've already learned, deep learning is reliant on the use of neural networks. These networks have been designed with the human brain in mind and if you compare a diagram of the brain with one of an artificial neural network (ANN), you will see some strong similarities.

What is a Neural Network?

Basically, a neural network can be described as a system patterned to operate like the human brain. The artificial neural network (ANN) is made up of layers of interconnected neurons that can receive a series of inputs and weights. It will take the data and perform a series of mathematical computations to come up with an output or result that can be similar to that of the biological brain.

A neural network is comprised of four components:

- Neurons

- Topology – this is the connective path between the different neurons

- Weights

- Learning Algorithm

While the function of an ANN is to mimic the human brain, it cannot do so exactly. One of the reasons for this is because the ANN is designed with thousands of neurons whereas the human brain consists of billions. So, there is the possibility that it will learn in a similar way to copy the human mind, but it is far from a perfect replication of the real deal.

The Structure of a Neural Network

Still, there are many functions that an ANN can perform that can be applied in a number of ways. Let's take a look at a diagram of a biological neuron found in a human brain and compare it.

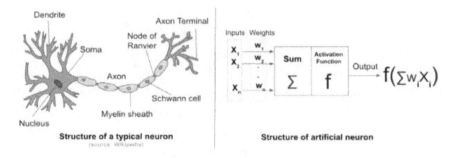

Structure of a typical neuron
(source: Wikipedia)

Structure of artificial neuron

In a biological neural network, the neurons consist of a cell nucleus that can receive input from the billions of other neurons in the network. This is done through a series of input terminals called dendrites (a group of dendrites together is referred to as a dendrite tree), which receives different types of signals from other neurons in the network. The signals can be excitatory or inhibitory in nature and are delivered via an electrochemical exchange of neurotransmitters.

How strong these input signals are will depend on several factors including the amplitude of the action coming from the previous neuron and the conductivity of the ion channels that are feeding the dendrites. The ion channels allow for the flow of electrical signals passing through the neuron's membrane or outer shell.

When signals are frequent or are of a larger magnitude, they generally have a much better conductivity in the ion channels so the signal is easier to propagate.

Depending on the type of signal received, the neuron will respond with either a message to activate or to inhibit. In other words, it will be told to turn on or turn off. Each neuron contains an electrochemical threshold, which determines whether the data received is sufficient enough to turn on the neuron or not. The result of all this activity is then sent to other neurons and the process continues.

Learning with the human brain is achieved by making tiny little adjustments to an existing configuration of neurons. Each configuration is created based on specific details before any learning can begin. How strong the connection of the neurons are, or the weights, are not random nor does the brain's topology have an effect on them.

Over time though, the strength of these connections will change based on their adjusting formation that affects both the topology and weights. Each time an adjustment is made learning happens. In the human brain, all of this happens automatically, in an instant. We watch this in babies as they learn to walk, talk, and play. Throughout our lives, we meet and get to know new people and our brains are capable of distinguishing one person from another based on numerous factors. The way they look, how they sound, their walk, etc. Every time we learn something new our brain makes these small adjustments to the neural networks and the results are stored as memories.

This function is completed in all sorts of tasks and environments. We can recognize objects, process sounds, and speech patterns. None of these skills are learned automatically but are developed slowly and repeatedly over extended periods of time. Each time the brain literally rewires itself to perfect the task it has been challenged to do.

Evidence of this was discovered through a series of experiments on animals. Their eyes were forced to remain closed for two months during their developmental stage while researchers observed the changes in the animal's visual cortex. After the two months, the animal's eyes were allowed to open but they were no longer receptive to light. In the cells and in the brain the eye had physically changed and was no longer able to function. We've now seen the same thing happening in humans. Studies have revealed that those who spend the majority of their lives in cities are found to be more sensitive to parallel lines and sharp edges, whereas those who spend the majority of their time in rural areas have eyes that are more sensitive to smooth textures.

How Learning Happens in ANNs

In artificial neural networks, the training starts with a fixed topology specifically chosen to address a certain problem. These topologies do not change with time and their weights are adjusted at random. This is done with the use of an optimization algorithm used to map the formation of input stimuli into a single cluster in order to get the desired result.

However, it is possible for ANNs to learn or to be fine-tuned based on their pre-existing representation. The process involves making adjustments to the previous weights from its original topology. This process does not happen as quickly as the human brain does but it does so at a very slow learning weight as it reacts to the newly supplied input data.

This training occurs when the weight update process starts to send data through the neural network. It measures the outcome and adjusts the weights according to the results. The weights are generally "pushed" in the direction that is most likely to improve the performance of the objective. So, an ANN designed to recognize objects will take the feedback and adjust the weights accordingly. This type of programming can be compared to a child who is learning how to recognize certain things. It is more a trial and error approach. After each failed attempt, his brain will analyze the feedback, and then take a different direction the next time.

This will be repeated until the child reaches the desired result. An ANN works the same general way. It is first given stimuli or data that has a known response along with a learning regime that will make adjustments in an attempt to maximize accuracy.

Once the machine has learned, it can then use the experience and apply it to new stimuli, even if it is something it has never been exposed to before. The more problems the machine has to solve, the faster it will be able to learn how to tackle new ones because the connections will become much more defined.

The More Exposure – The Better

While up until recently we weren't able to explain it scientifically, we have known for centuries that the more you expose a child to the world, the faster they learn. This is true, even when the learning process is an unpleasant experience. In fact, when the learning process is painful, the feedback they receive is even more memorable. With an ANN the same could be true. When an ANN is exposed to a variety of stimuli, the fine-tuning process can ensure that it is not being overly exposed to a single thread of processing.

With each additional type of stimuli, the network can "learn" how to classify new stimuli it will receive in the future. The basic principle behind this is based on the "Black Swan Theory," in the human brain and in ANNs if they have only been exposed to one type of stimuli it is impossible for them to conceive of another type of stimuli. For centuries, people had concluded that all swans were white because there had been no recorded facts of a swan of any other color. In other words, no one had seen or been exposed to a swan that was not white. However, later a Dutch explorer by the name of Willem de Vlamingh actually saw a group of black swans in Western Australia. Once he was exposed to this new stimuli, he had to adjust his understanding and create a new element of classifying them. If an ANN is only fed a limited stream of input, it cannot learn to classify other data that it has not been exposed to.

Its ability to draw knowledge from what it has learned is a huge stride in computer science. It allows machines to solve problems across all spectrums with a phenomenal array of applications, often with the ability to find a better solution than what would normally be achieved.

While this is a major advancement that far surpasses anything that machines have been able to do before, it is safe to conclude that this type of technology is still in its early stages. They still have a long way to go before they are capable of even coming close to being able to do what the human brain can do. Their topology is much too basic, they're learning algorithms are as of now, extremely naïve.

Still, as technology continues to advance, ANNs will continue to learn how to solve problems more effectively and face many more unknown issues in the future. Already these devices have been able to outperform human analysts in accuracy and speed in a number of areas. It is believed that one day, they will be able to multitask like humans and mimic some of the most impressive human minds in all manner of things. But that goal is now many years in the future.

Input, Hidden, and Output Layers

Now, let's look a little closer at how these neural networks work. Even someone who is not computer savvy understands that computers use processors and memory to perform complex computations. For years, man has been astounded by the speed at which these machines can calculate a result. This has been going on for decades with huge success. Think of your calculator you carry around with you all the time. Computation is a given in the world of machines. But now, because of the introduction of neural networks, a whole new approach to problem-solving has begun.

To understand this better, we must first know that a computer consists of 10^9 transistors with a switching time of 10^9 seconds. What does that mean? Transistors are tiny little switches that are triggered by electrical impulses. These are the basic building blocks used in microchips and other computer devices. Compare that to the human brain, which has 10^{11} neurons, but they have a switching time of only 10^3 seconds.

The neurons in the human brain can be compared to the human nervous system, which has three different parts. The primary part is the brain or the nerve center, which is constantly receiving input it needs to process before making decisions. Input is received and sent to the nerve center, which processes all the data, analyzes it, and sends out instructions to the rest of the body.

- Data is received from the 5 senses.

- The central nervous system analyzes it and sends out instructions on how to respond.

- The body receives instructions from the brain and executes the appropriate action.

Now let's make another comparison with the machine to see how input differs. In a human brain:

- Synapses are at the most basic level and are completely reliant on molecules and ions for their actions.

- A neural microcircuit assigns a group of neurotransmitters to perform a particular operation

- The neural microcircuits are collected together to create subunits found in the dendrite trees

- Each neuron is capable of holding several of these dendrite subunits.

- These neural groupings work together to perform instructed operations.

- Interregional circuits create pathways, topographic maps of the cerebrum.

- The sensory system is the point where the topographic maps interrupt certain forms of conduct.

What is an Output Layer?

At the opposite end of the spectrum, a layer sits at the highest-level building block of the deep learning world. It is basically a container that receives the input and then adapts it with many of the non-linear functions and then passes the results on to the next layer. Layers are usually uniform in structure and can hold only one type of activation. This makes it easy to compare that layer to another part of the same network.

To make this easier to understand think of the first layer as the input layer and the last layer as the output layer.

What is a Unit?

A unit can be found in both input and output layers. It is simply the activation function where the inputs are adjusted using a nonlinear format. In most cases, a unit will have a number of income connections as well as some outgoing connections.

These neural networks calculate the weighted sum of all of the input, adjusts for bias, and then determines whether the data justifies factoring it in the decision or not. This decision is determined by checking the value that a neuron produces before deciding if an outside connection should be included.

Units are extremely complex, and a single unit can have numerous activation functions in it. The neurons contained in any given layer can receive similar functions or enactment work. The type of enactment utilized will be consistent across that specific layer.

Hidden Layers

A neural network consists of a massive number of artificial neurons (the units) that are stacked up in a series of layers. All of these neurons are interconnected through an extremely complex web. We've already discussed the input layer, which makes up the foundation of the entire network and the output layer, which performs the calculations and adapts the data to get a result. But there is most likely a number of hidden layers that lie between input and output layers.

Each neuron located in a hidden layer is also fully connected to all of the neurons in the previous layer as well as all the neurons in the following layer. It is only the input layer that does not need to modify the data received. Its sole responsibility is to receive the data from the environment. In essence, it is purely an information layer.

The hidden layer, however, must copy that data and distribute it to all the nodes it is connected to within the structure where it will perform the calculations needed to determine what to do with the information received.

The output layer performs any computations and then transmits instructions to the external environment.

Types of Neural Networks

There are several types of neural networks depending on when they were created and the extent of their complexity. The oldest of these neural networks and the simplest is the perceptron. The machine introduced in 1958, was capable of learning by means of input vectors assigned to different classes of data.

Every piece of data received has to be scaled up or down based on how important it is to the task. When a signal comes in, it is first multiplied by a predetermined weight value. So, if a neuron receives three different inputs, then that neuron will have three weights assigned to it; each can be adjusted individually.

When the computer is learning, the computer will determine the weight value based on the number of errors it made from its last test.

Next, these modified input signals are summed up to create a single value for each of the neurons. An additional computation is performed called the "bias" and is also added to the sum. After the machine learns, all the weights and biases shift so that the next result will be a little bit closer to what is the expected output demonstrating that it has actually learned from the exercise.

In the final phase, the result of the calculations is transformed into an output signal, which is then fed to the activation function and sent out to the external environment.

In perceptron, this is a very basic binary function that can produce only two possible results.

$$f(x) = \{1 \text{ if } w \cdot x + b > 0, 0 \text{ otherwise}\}$$

Based on this formula, the function will result in a 1 if the input is positive but if the input is negative, the return will be 0. Any neuron with a function like this one is a perceptron.

To train a perceptron requires the use of several preparation tests and determining the yield for each one. After each test is completed, the weights are rebalanced in a path so that it will reduce the yield error.

Adaline

The Adaline neural network (ADAptive LINear Element) followed perceptron. The general rule with Adaline sometimes called the delta rule is designed to minimize the number of output errors using a gradient descent.

After a training pattern has been completed, the weights are corrected in proportion to the error percentage. The primary difference between Adaline and perceptron is the way the output applies the learning rule. In perceptron, it uses the output of the threshold function learning. However, with ADALINE, it uses the output values of -1 or +1.

The delta rule states that for a given input vector, the output vector must be compared to the correct answer. If the difference is zero, the machine did not learn. If the zero is anything else, the weights need to be adjusted as an effort to lower the difference.

The delta rule makes use of the difference between the target output values and the obtained activation. In simple terms, it compares the desired output values of the machine with the obtained activation to determine learning. It disregards perceptron's threshold activation function and instead uses a linear sum of products to calculate the activation function of the output neuron.

Throughout the training process, the strength of the connections within the network is adjusted to reduce the difference between the two values. The reason for the shift was because the threshold activation function used with perceptron could not be used in gradient descent learning needed in programs that followed. The adjustment of the values at the end of each lesson could not get progressively closer to the target with this method. However, the linear activation used with Madeline made room for error calculations to yield outputs that could be adjusted with each lesson.

How do Algorithms Work?

There is a basic principle that applies to all supervised machine learning algorithms that allow them to perform predictive modeling. The focus of each algorithm is to take the target function (f) and create a map that takes the machine from the input variable (x) to the output variable (Y). The resulting algorithm will look like this:

$$Y = f(x)$$

In this basic algorithm, the task is to make predictions about the future (Y) with examples of input variables (x).

While this formula looks on the surface to be very simple, it becomes extremely complicated when you do not know the form of function f. If this variable was known, there would be no need for the machine to learn it. Instead, it would use it in the formula to get the desired result.

There is another element that makes performing this calculation even more complicated. The algorithm must also allow for errors (e) that are completely independent of the input data (x), so the formula must be adjusted.

$$Y = f(x) + e$$

There are a number of variables that could represent e. The machine may not have enough attributes to characterize the best mapping solution. With this type of error, no matter how good the machine is at making estimates, it will never be able to reduce that error.

Algorithms like these make it possible for machines to learn and to make predictions. This is termed "predictive analytics." In general, machine learning algorithms are designed to estimate a mapping function of several output variables when they are applied to the given input variables.

With these algorithms, the machine can learn to make different assumptions based on the formula of its underlying function. If the machine does not have enough data to generate a reasonable assumption, it will not be able to learn no matter how well it performs its programmed tasks. Without algorithms carefully designed to target the task at hand, machine learning would not be what it has become today.

Chapter 4:
Presentation of Deep Learning

While the primary purpose of deep learning is applied to ANNs, its development has many more applications where it can be used. Since scientists first realized how many different ways these neural networks can be applied, research has begun in a wide range of areas creating systems that go far beyond the artificial.

These new and innovative machines represent the future of deep learning and are expected to eventually replace the artificial neural networks in use today.

This is a phenomenal accomplishment in the history of mankind, however, as advanced as they are, they still have many limitations; one being their immense size. They require many systems in order for them to function properly but their list of tasks they can perform is very small. Think of it in terms of the first computers invented. They were large in size (some taking up an entire room) but the number of functions they could perform was actually quite limited.

The same could be said for these deep learning machines today. The goal for the future is to create a type of artificial intelligence that requires only minimal human input and can perform a vast number of functions. This was the underlying purpose of deep learning.

The deep neural network is the next evolutionary step of the ANN. The machines used are considerably smaller but with the capability of performing even more complex functions that go far beyond the capabilities of the ANNs. Deep neural networks are targeted to have a more usable program that will allow the machines to work effectively and efficiently without consuming so much space and energy.

To achieve this deep neural network of the future, several things had to change.

GPUs/CPUs

Most of us are familiar with CPUs (central processing units). We may not know exactly what it is, but we know it represents the brains of our personal computer systems. For years, the CPU was both the heart and the brain of the computer.

In time, however, the CPU was improved upon with the aid of another computer part that was not so familiar. The graphics processing unit or the GPU. In every computer, there are chips responsible for displaying images on the computer monitor and a GPU is one of the most powerful chips you have. While these chips have the same function, some are not as effective as others. Some will provide only the most basic of graphics and others will function on a much higher level.

The GPU is one of those components of your computer which goes much further than displaying a clear picture of a computer game. Their role does not stop at displaying graphics, they can be programmed and perform computations separate from the CPU in any system. Deep learning uses GPUs to address many of the limitations that the ANNs have faced since their inception.

For the most part, GPUs were initially designed for use in computer games but because of their immense power they have far exceeded expectations and have quickly been adapted for other uses that have been applied in a number of ways.

How is the GPU Designed?

To get better graphics on your computer, you need a better graphics card, a basic truth that most people can readily understand. At its most basic level, a GPU differs from a CPU in that while they perform basically the same function but with entirely different architectures. Both machines will receive a problem in the form of zeros and ones (binary code) and both will solve the problem quickly.

However, the way they are designed is where they part ways. CPUs are designed with hundreds of simple cores and GPUs have thousands. When you compare this difference in computers you can understand it more clearly. The top of the line computer, the Mac Pro, has a six-core processor while the NVidia GTX 980 graphics card has more than 2000. This allows for clearer pictures, better resolution, and a host of other benefits.

There are other differences beyond having more core. You can think of the CPU as a device that can perform lots of easy tasks that it can complete quickly and efficiently. On a computer system, it can solve geometrical equations or shade in a picture. The GPU, on the other hand, is better suited for complex tasks and problem-solving. This is why it is so much more practical to use with artificial intelligence.

Today's advanced neural networks make use of a number of systems to keep them running including algorithms and GPUs. As a result, deep learning can be adapted to all sorts of industries to help solve many problems that may or may not apply to artificial intelligence. It is already being used in speech recognition, language processing, and computer vision.

Because GPUs are a major component of machines, it can be adapted to a wide variety of situations using many layers of data to solve a host of problems. Depending on the different designs and strategies used, GPUs can help in three different classifications of deep learning.

- **Unsupervised or Generative Learning**

   This type of learning is meant to capture obvious images for pattern analysis at times when no target data is available.

- **Supervised Deep Learning**

   These are used to discern and classify different patterns.

- **Hybrid Deep Networks**

   These are designed to distinguish between different elements in the data. The objective of hybrid deep networks can be improved when used with supervised learning and are primarily used to analyze different parameters in the input data.

Deep Learning Methods

Another aspect of deep learning is something called Dynamic Programming. This allows the machine to tackle certain problems with the use of algorithms based on a recurrent formula and a starting state. A "state" is a way to describe a particular situation or problem the machine must solve. A sub-solution is then constructed from any previously found ones in the system. DP algorithms are a fundamental part of the framework in neural networks and graphical models.

- **Unsupervised Learning with SL & RL**

  This deep learning method is regularly used when encoding input data is needed. Data streams like video or speech need to be encoded into a form that is better geared towards machine learning. These codes describe the initial data in a manner that reduces redundancy, so it can be fed into SL or RL machines. These machines usually have a much smaller search space and cannot manage such large quantities of raw data.

- **Back Propagation**

  This is simply a method that allows the system to compute the partial gradients of a function. When the machine solves an optimization problem with a gradient-based method, it must also compute the function each time it repeats. To compute the gradient, the machine can either use analytic differentiation: it knows the form of the function and simply needs to compute the derivatives, or it can use the approximate differentiation using finite differences.

- **Stochastic Gradient Descent**

  This is a very intuitive way to create a gradient descent. Imagine looking at a river as it flows from the top of a mountain. The goal of the machine is to determine exactly where the river is going and the path it is going to take. To accomplish this the machine needs to know certain elements of the problem: the terrain of the mountain, lowest point of the foothill, the curvature of the hills. In machine learning, the input point (the very top of the hill) may be the only input it has to solve the problem. As it tries to work out the solution, it will label dips and valleys as local minima solutions, which it will have to navigate to get around. The output could be any number of possible paths the river might take. Each time it addresses this problem it may reach its final destination in a completely different manner each time.

- **Learning Rate Decay**

  To improve on the Stochastic Gradient Descent, there is the Learning Rate Decay method. This method is often used to reduce the learning rate over a period of time. It allows the machine to make large changes at the start of a training test by using larger learning rate values and decreasing them according to the weights assigned in the training procedure. It may lower the learning rate based on the epoch or by using punctuated large drops at specific epochs.

- **Occam's Razor**

  This method works in the simpler problems rather than the complex. The concept of the possible solutions, the machine will select the data with the simplest explanation available. Given the input, the machine will determine a list of possible solutions to the problem. A good way to think of it is to imagine a patient going to the doctor complaining of a headache and a sore throat. There are several medical conditions that can explain a headache, a brain tumor, an aneurysm, a stroke. There are also several possibilities that can explain a sore throat, an infection or a virus. The machine would compare all of these solutions and filter out those that explain only one symptom and not both. Then it will finally filter out the conditions that are extreme and narrow it down to the simplest one. A cold or the flu would explain both symptoms.

There are many more methods that can be applied to deep learning. Because of their fast speeds and impressive computational power, they have been at the heart of machine learning for years. With these additions to machines, learning can be accelerated to work at least 50x faster.

Chapter 5:
Multilayer Perceptron

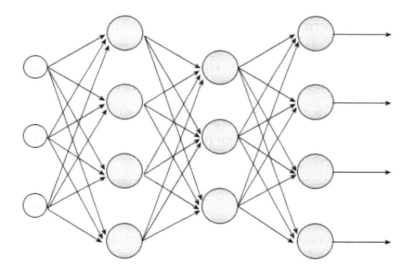

Multilayer Perceptron or MLP is normally used when the machine has access to standard data. This would be any type of data contained in a table format with rows and columns. The factors (rows and columns) in these algorithms are interchangeable so the machine can switch a row for a column or vice-versa without having the change the value of the information it contains.

An MLP can take the input and change it using a learned non-linear transformation. The change can effectively project the input data into an area where it can be separated into layers.

The middle layer or the hidden layer is sufficient enough to create an MLP.

How it Works

When training MLPs there are a few things that must be kept in mind. First, there are a number of hyperparameters that cannot be enhanced or improved with gradient descent. So, finding these hyperparameters isn't a simple problem to solve. First, they can't be easily optimized nor can the machine apply gradient strategies to them. The trick is to find these hyperparameters in the neural network.

You can discern from its name that a Multilayer perceptron consists of more than one perceptron. They have an input layer that receives a signal, an output layer to make a prediction, and a varying number of hidden layers that will run the computations.

MLPs are usually used to solve supervised learning problems. They are trained with a set of input/output pairs and will model the dependencies that exist between the inputs and the outputs. During the training, adjustments are made to the weights and biases as it tries to reduce the error rate.

MLPs are considered feedforward networks and they work in a similar fashion to a game of tennis. They have two functions, which they switch back and forth. Each function is a guess and the next function is the answer. Since every guess represents a test of what they have assumed to be the correct answer the response is the feedback informing the machine that it is right or wrong.

With the forward pass, the signal moves from the input layer, cross the net (the hidden layers) to the output layer. When it hits the ground, it is measured and the truth is returned.

Backpropagation

There is another type of signal pass that is used with MLPs. It is called the backpropagation and it applies the chain rule of calculus, partial derivatives of an error function, along with the weights and biases. In this process, determining the differentiation between all the elements will produce a gradient or a landscape of different errors. That taken along with the parameters can be adjusted with each pass taking it one step closer to the minimum error percentage.

With MLP, the back and forth passes will continue until the machine reaches a point where it cannot get any lower. This is called the point of convergence.

To properly complete a backpropagation, three things are needed:

1. A data set in both input and output pairs where x is the input and y is the desired output.

2. Feedforward neural networks where the layers are all completely connected.

3. An error function that calculates the output of the input data given.

This type of neural network requires the machine to calculate the gradient of error with weights and biases for each pass until a solution is reached.

Applications

There are several applications where this type of machine learning can be very effective.

Function approximation where the network learns how to estimate the value of a particular function. Data is stored in the machine or fed to it and the system processes it to identify a pattern.

Time series prediction the network learns how to predict a value using data obtained during a specific time frame. This application is most often used in stock markets and similar fields where anticipating future moves are needed.

Language Processing machines learn to decipher spoken language with language modeling. The program uses deep learning networks and is capable of understanding native language in such a way that they can actually have basic conversations with participants. They can communicate rationally for extended periods of time. This application is so advanced that these machines are capable of understanding jokes, rephrasing expressions, and adapting to a wide range of verbal communications. You may have already used one of these applications. If you've ever used Google Translate online, you understand the concept.

Long/Short Term Memory Networks are used in backpropagation where the gradient signal is multiplied numerous times by the weight matrix. If the weights in a particular matrix are very small, it can result in a situation commonly referred to as vanishing gradients because the gradient signals can diminish to the point where the learning has slowed down so much that it cannot continue.

On the other hand, it can become so complex that the task can create long-term dependencies on the data. This can end up in a situation where the signal becomes so large that learning cannot be contained, and you end up with something referred to as exploding gradients.

These challenges are addressed with the use of the Long/Short Term Memory Networks, which utilize a new structure called the memory cell. This cell consists of four major components.

1. An input gate

2. A neuron that has a self-recurrent connection

3. A forget gate

4. An output gate

The neuron with the self-recurrent link comes with a weight of 1.0 and assures that the memory cell remains constant from one time to the next. The other gates modulate interactions that happen between the memory cell and the environment. The cell's input gate can allow a signal to enter and alter the status of the memory cell or block it altogether, but the output gate can permit the status of the memory cell to have an impact on other neurons on the network or block it from doing so. The role of the forget gate is to modulate the self-recurrent connection and allow the cell to forget its previous status if needed.

Chapter 6:
Convolutional Neural Networks

Convolutional neural networks use many types of identical copies of the same neuron. This makes it possible for the network to learn a neuron one time and then apply it in a number of different situations, thus simplifying the overall learning process and lowering the chance of machine error.

These systems were inspired by the biological processes found in the brains of living beings. It was made to mimic the design of the neurons in the visual cortex. In this type of neural network, individual cortical neurons respond to stimuli only within a limited visual field. Collectively, the visual field of many different neurons can efficiently cover the entire visual field.

CNN's are basically a way to classify neural networks that have already proved to be very powerful in specialized fields like image recognition and classification. These networks can identify faces, objects, and traffic signs by controlling how machines and self-driving cars see.

CNN's are made up of several different convolutional and sub-sampling layers all connected together. The input layer is represented by the formula:

$$m \times m \times r \text{ picture}$$

In this formula, the m is equal to the height and the width of a picture and r represents the number of color channels. The convolutional or the input layer will have k filters sized with the formula

$$n \times n \times q$$

With this formula, n is less than the dimensions of the image and q can be either equal or of a smaller size. This factor could shift with every filter. The number of filters allows for the ascent to any locally associated filters, including maps.

Maps can then be sub-sampled with a mean or max pooling that spreads out over a contiguous region using the formula

$$p \times p$$

In this case, p has to be a value between 2 and 5 depending on the size of the input.

Beyond the convoluted layers, there could be any number of connected hidden layers. These connected layers can be difficult to distinguish from the layers in a multilayer neural system.

In a CNN, each layer in the arrangement can change a single volume of activation through a differentiable function. The layers may be labeled as the convolutional or input layer, a pooling layer, and a fully connected layer. These layers could all be stacked to create a highly complex network.

Chapter 7:
How Deep Learning Can Be Used

With the growing emergence of artificial intelligence and deep learning, there is more than enough opportunities for this science to grow and expand beyond its present boundaries. There are three noteworthy events that have been instrumental in projecting this type of technology forward and into the world's consciousness.

The ability of machines to learn and be trained is an important significance for our future. As a result, the framework that has begun to overtake the traditional and outdated technologies in various fields has made it possible for humans to take immense strides in their progress. This can be great news for some people and may cause trouble for others, but the reality is that this technology is here to stay.

Still, like every other modern advancement in the world, people and businesses alike are now learning how to use deep learning to solve a host of real-world problems. However, there are fundamental elements in how deep learning is used and applied in these situations that cannot be ignored.

Pre-training

In machine learning, the process does not focus on collecting numerous datasets. Rather, the machines do the exact opposite. When comparing deep learning techniques to other methods it is important to establish a consistent measure that determines which strategy works better on the same or similar evaluation period. A general rule of thumb is to measure the performance of each strategy based on a set number of datasets using a regular evaluation period.

The problem with this is that in real-world situations, the result is not about how to get an extra percentage out of the error rate but is more focused on building a better robot so to speak. This means that labeling training strategies and highlighting which algorithm used can help the machine to learn better.

To solve many real-world problems, this can turn out to be a very expensive process.

For example, in the field of medicine, a machine designed to detect lymph nodes in the human body by analyzing tomography images (or CT scans) is already in use. This is an extremely time-consuming task because the machine must recognize very small structures. It can also be very expensive as well. Based on the assumption that a radiologist earns around $100/hr and a CT scan can only produce 4 images an hour the cost of such a test could easily run up to $10,000 to get enough images for a proper diagnosis.

Add to that the consultation fee for having an additional doctor on hand to confirm the diagnosis, acquiring sufficient data to give an accurate diagnosis could easily go beyond the quarter of a million mark. That is just for diagnosis only; it does not include any treatment options that will come later.

Credit History

Deep learning is also used in determining your credit score. Machines can learn to analyze patterns to determine who has the highest risk of defaulting on their loan before credit is issued to them. Companies that issue loans to anyone are at the highest risk of finding someone who will default on their loan. This makes issuing credit a very expensive venture. Machines that can learn to analyze spending patterns, payment history, and financial health can make sure that those risks are greatly reduced.

In Computer Games

You've probably already heard about computers that have learned how to play chess or other games. In this type of learning, the pixels on the screen form the basis of the game. The goal and the most complicated task the machine must do is to break through the Deep Mind.

Depending on how complex the game is there are many elements to game playing that the computer has to learn. It will have to navigate through environments, different storylines, character behavior, and other rules in order to master the game.

With it comes to pre-training, the fine-tuning segment learns how to quantify different classes and make the necessary adjustments. Neural networks are pre-trained based on specified datasets and then are fine-tuned to fit within the parameters of a unique problem. Each problem has its own set of different anomalies. The input data informs the machine exactly which layer needs to be adjusted and the learning rates are reset, usually a little higher than the last layer.

In Education

The focus of education is to reach a point where you outperform learning models regardless of the model you choose. When functioning with real-world applications it is not always easy to design a model that functions as it should. It is important that when a learning machine makes an error that it can understand how and why it did so. It must have some ability to ascertain why a specific model did better than any other previous solution, and it is extremely important that you understand that the existing model in use cannot be tricked.

In the Movie Industry

Machine learning is now capable of adding sounds to silent video. The framework was designed to analyze 1000 examples of video playing with a drumstick beating on different surfaces to create different sounds. The machine then studies the video and compares it to a database of pre-recorded sounds and matches the right sound with the scene in the video. The finished scene was then tested for accuracy with humans who were asked to determine which video was the real silent film and which one was matched with sounds added in by computer.

Automatic Language Translation

This type of deep learning trains machines to identify spoken words, expressions, and sentences in an input language and then translate it into a target language. Automatic translation by machines is not a new application but deep learning has been able to add a whole new element to machine translating. It can now automatically translate written text both in printed form and handwritten form and it can also translate images.

Text translation is performed without the use of preprocessing, allowing the algorithms the freedom to learn from the interdependencies that exist between words and then mapping them to the target language.

This function is usually done with the convolutional neural networks because of their ability to identify and recognize all sorts of images. These machines can recognize letters in text, translate them, and then immediately send the translated text to its destination.

Images can also be translated by classifying objects in a photograph as a single set of known objects stored in its memory. Object detection includes being able to identify one or more objects in a photograph and drawing and labeling a box around them.

Handwriting Generation

Probably one of the most impressive applications of deep learning is the ability machines now have to produce handwriting. The machine learns by analyzing a collection of handwriting samples and then produces its own handwritten word or phrase. This is done by inputting a series of coordinates using a digital pen to create its own handwriting samples.

Once the machine has learned the images of samples, it studies the relationship that exists between the pen and the letters to create a new set of handwritten samples to choose from. This may not seem very amazing to you, but the machine can actually learn different handwriting styles and then mimic them back to you.

There are many more uses for deep learning that are in play today. Without your realizing it, you're coming in direct contact with deep learning machines every day. When you turn on your TV, when you make a purchase, use your credit, or even when you go out to eat. Deep learning has already permeated every part of human life and is poised to take us into a whole new era for the world. Ever wonder what deep learning has in store for the future?

Chapter 8:
Deep Learning and the Future

While deep learning is slowly making inroads into our everyday lives, there is much more of it in our future to look forward to. It is a rapidly growing form of technology and as a result, we can realistically expect to see much more of it in the years to come. It will continue to be integrated into ways we are familiar with but more importantly, in ways that we may not have yet thought of.

Considering what we already know about neural networks and the steady stream of research projects popping up all across the globe, we don't really need a machine that can learn to predict what the future holds. Perhaps everything we expect may not pan out, but we can be certain that whatever it is, someone, somewhere is already working on it. Let's take a look at some of the predictions others have made about the future of deep learning to see where we're going.

A Function for the General Population

Some expect that one-day deep learning and artificial intelligence will be available for the general population in much the same way as the personal computer is now in nearly every household. Already, people are working on using this technology to build smart homes that will anticipate your every need, self-driving cars are just one generation away, and computer technology that will anticipate your every move.

Its Ability Will Only Expand

The capabilities of deep learning will improve opening up even more doors to functions that will make life easier. No doubt deep learning can do amazing things today, but it is still a far cry from truly thinking like a human brain. As its technology and the science behind it grows, we can expect whole new forms of learning to be presented with models that will move away from the limitations it now holds. Today, deep learning is limited to recognition, classifications, computations, and identification. Eventually, it will be able to reason like the human mind and will be capable of abstract thinking as well. When that happens the implications that will follow will be immense.

They Will Have More Autonomy

Right now, all forms of deep learning need some involvement from humans to function. In supervised learning, the machine must be fed data and tested based on parameters set by humans. Even in unsupervised learning, these machines need some input from humans to start their program and utilize inputted data.

In the future, these machines could eventually reach the point where they can create the next generation of their technology themselves, program them completely without the aid of human interference. As they continue to learn and to store the information they have acquired, accessing it when needed, it is highly possible that this reusable knowledge will help them to design and create their own machine learning and adapt it to their own needs.

There Will be a Move Away from Models

Right now, a principal part of deep learning is the different models in existence. In the future, it is expected that the models we see in use today will one day become computer programs that will be able to adapt to all sorts of situations whether pre-programmed for it or not.

More Advancements in Medical Technology

It is feasible that every medical lab in the country will be equipped with learning machines that will be able to diagnose illnesses, test lab results, learn how to perform surgery, or dispense with medication, all without human interaction. Imagine a world where a machine can analyze your DNA samples to help doctors to learn about your potential for medical risks or to determine if you have a gene for Alzheimer's or some other illness. This knowledge would allow you to take steps ahead of time in order to stop the disease from ever happening.

Biomechanics

The future may also usher in a new era of biomechanics. Already nanotechnology is able to create limbs and other body parts for patient use. Instead of having to use a donor's heart, these tiny learning machines could be able to create a heart for you in a lab. An artificially created limb can be taught to perform like the real limbs would.

Better Mobile Technology

Can you make a smartphone any smarter? With deep learning, anything is possible. Mobile technology could literally become a personal virtual assistant, scheduling appointments, performing personal tasks, and managing your life overall. If you had the freedom away from such mundane chores you will then be free to engage in a host of other activities that you haven't been able to find the time for.

Machines Performing Mundane Tasks

One day, machines will perform the basic and more mundane tasks that humans now have to do. Self-driving trucks will come to your neighborhood will pick up your garbage every week, they will clean your home, prepare your meals, and even tidy up your home.

They Will Have Bigger Capabilities

As more algorithms are introduced, deep learning can only expand. This means there will be more automation, so each machine will be able to perform more than one task. Each layer of the neural networks can introduce a whole new feature to add to their abilities. In time, you'll have an AI that's sole responsibilities are to take care of you.

The reality is that we don't know exactly what the future holds or what to expect, but if history tells us anything, we all understand that this type of technology has a very long and prosperous future. We may not ever see the day when Sarah Conner has to fight off the Terminator and we are far from the threat of world domination by machines, but we can fully and realistically expect that machines will slowly become a major part of our lives.

We may not see it in our lifetime, but the time will come when machines will change the way live, work and play in a myriad of different ways. Every day, we are learning more about this new and exciting technology and what it can do for us. One thing for sure, our future looks bright and promising with deep learning on the horizon we have many good things to look forward to.

Conclusion

Living in today's modern age can be very exciting. We exist at a time that only a half-century ago was the stuff of science fiction. Today, with deep learning at the core of computer science we have the ability to do things never thought possible.

Whether you're reading this book out of curiosity or if you're seriously considering playing a significant role in the future of this new technology, we hope that we have been able to at least peak your interest in this subject and what it means for all of us.

We have made every attempt to keep the language simple enough for the layman to understand but technical enough not to bore those who have a base knowledge of the subject. Still, sad to say, we've only touched on the subject in these pages. Even though these few pages could not take you into the depths of the world of deep science we have been able to give you a basic overview of the subject and how it came about. We've talked about what foundation knowledge you need to get started.

You learned about neural networks, what they mean and how they work and some of the different types of networks and how they can be used in our modern and progressive world. Then we discuss the presentation of deep learning, multilayer perceptron's, and convolutional neural networks. All different aspects of the same technology.

No doubt, you have a lot to think about when it comes to deep learning. It is the technology that lies at the very heart of machine learning and artificial intelligence. These amazing programs, patterned after the human brain and the way it works are opening all sorts of new doors to the future. You don't have to be a scientist, mathematician, or a computer technician to see the possibilities. There is more than enough room to grow and whether you plan to work someday in this field or you're looking to use it in your personal life, this technology is introducing us to a completely new way of life.

We hope that by now, you understand how those ads keep popping up when you're searching the Internet, how Netflix knows exactly what movies you're going to like, or how that one company seems to find you wherever you go. You now understand how Google translate can translate languages in an instant and you understand how Twitter has the capacity to comprehend and analyze everything you post with them.

Deep learning is a very complex subject and it may be difficult to understand. If that's you, don't feel discouraged. Keep this book close by and read it in small bites. Eventually, you will grasp its meaning and if you're seriously interested, don't be afraid to reach out for more knowledge. Thank you for walking with us into the world of machine learning, artificial intelligence, and deep learning. We hope that you enjoyed it and will be ready to come back for more soon.

Finally, if you found this book useful in any way, a review on Amazon is always appreciated!

www.ingramcontent.com/pod-product-compliance
Lightning Source LLC
Chambersburg PA
CBHW071135050326
40690CB00008B/1477